Powered On: A State of Mind

AF530055

Verses Kindler Publication

Verses Kindler Publication

Website: www.verseskindlerpublication.com

© Copyright, 2025 – Samit Doshi

All rights reserved. No part of this book may be reproduced, stored in a retrieval system, or transmitted, in any form by any means, electronic, mechanical, magnetic, Optical, chemical, manual, photocopying, recording or otherwise, without the prior Written consent of its Writer.

Powered On: A State of Mind

By: Raj Mruthyunjayappa (Raj CM)

ISBN: 978-93-49532-22-9

1st Edition

Price: INR 299/$15

The opinions/ contents expressed in this book are solely of the author and do not represent the opinions/ standings/ Thoughts of PUBLISHER.

DISCLAIMER

Powered On: A State of Mind is authored by Raj Mruthyunjayappa (Raj CM). The entirety of this published work comprises the original content of the author, who has undertaken diligent efforts in its editing. The characters depicted herein may be fictitious or inspired by real events; however, they are not intended to cause offense or represent any prejudice against any caste or system. Any similarity to the names of actual individuals, locations, or institutions is purely coincidental and serves the narrative. The author bears sole responsibility for the originality of this work; the publisher assumes no liability thereof.

Index

Chapter 1: The Power On Mindset

"Power On", What It Really Means

Every morning, there is a little thing, a powerful thing that determines the way that my day will turn out. It is that time when I wake up and my mind is still blurred, and I cannot move my body clearly. In that moment, I choose whether to "power on", not just get out of bed, not just start the day, but ignite. It's not about checking emails or glancing at my calendar. It's about choosing to step into energy, intention, and focus.

"Power On" is not a motivational catchphrase. It's a mindset. A personal switch. It's the internal decision to operate at full voltage, not as a reaction to the world, but as an initiation. You don't need a title or a team to flip that switch. In fact, the most powerful leaders are the ones who learned to "power on" before anyone gave them permission to lead others.

As I think of what the concept of leading is, I do not envision an individual giving order. I imagine a spark--a CB-tuneup of vitality, insight, and ambition which burns down around them. It is the type of presence that makes a room colder or warmer when entering the room. That power doesn't come from the org chart. It comes from inside.

Long before I ever led a team, I had to learn to lead myself, and that was the harder part.

The Moment I Switched On

My first job wasn't glamorous. I was part of a large HR team at a firm where most people didn't know each other's names, and hierarchies were carved in stone. On the surface, I was just another new joiner. No one was expecting innovation from me, just compliance and quiet efficiency.

And then came this small project. We were running into issues with an internal HR system that had been giving trouble for months. Everyone had accepted it as one of those annoying glitches you work around. It slowed things down, created confusion, and added more manual work. One afternoon, I stayed back late and started digging through old process manuals and data logs. I wasn't even supposed to. It just bothered me that no one was fixing it.

After a few hours of trial and error, I discovered a workaround, a small change that dramatically improved the way data was pulled from the system. The next morning, I presented it to my manager, half-expecting them to dismiss it. Instead, she lit up. She asked me to walk the entire team through it. A few weeks later, the updated process was rolled out company-wide.

I remember walking out of that meeting with a feeling I'll never forget. It wasn't pride. It was ignition.

I had switched on. Not because someone told me to. Not because it was in my job description. But because I chose to bring my energy into something that mattered. That was the first time I understood what it meant to "power on." It had nothing to do with power over others. It had everything to do with power within.

From "Me" to "We": The First Leap

The next shift came a year later, during a heated phase of cross-functional projects. I was leading a small task force and found myself constantly struggling to get everyone aligned. People were polite but disinterested. They showed up to meetings, nodded along, and left unchanged.

I kept wondering what I was missing. Why didn't they care as much as I did?

One afternoon, while reviewing an Excel dashboard I had spent hours perfecting, I had a jarring realization. I had built the dashboard for myself, for my satisfaction, my clarity, my recognition. I hadn't built it to enable others. The team didn't feel ownership because I hadn't invited them in.

Leadership, I realized, wasn't about being the one with the answers. It was about lighting the spark in others, creating shared clarity, shared ownership, and shared momentum.

That shift, from me to we, is the first true leap toward leadership. And it starts with managing your own energy. If you can't ignite yourself, how will you ever ignite a team?

The Anatomy of Energy

Let's pause here and unpack something vital: energy. We throw the word around a lot, but rarely stop to define it. What does it really mean to have energy?

For me, energy is not about caffeine or charisma. It's about intention with motion. It's the alignment of thought, emotion, and action. It's when your inner voltage is high enough to move things, to move yourself, your team, and eventually your organization.

But energy is not constant. It fluctuates. It gets drained, hijacked, or misplaced. And unless you understand how your energy system works, you'll find yourself running empty without realizing it.

Think of your brain as a machine that sorts activities into two boxes:

The "Happy Box": These are the things you love doing. They light you up. For some, it's music. For others, sports, writing, design, solving a tough problem, or having a great conversation. These activities give you energy because they align with your natural flow.

The "Duty Box": These are the tasks you have to do. Meetings, admin, reports, errands. They may not light you up, but they matter. You do them out of responsibility. But these drain energy, unless you approach them with purpose and anticipation.

The problem isn't the duty box. It's what comes after. When we overstay in tasks that drain us and fail to replenish through what energizes us, we fall into the third state, idling.

Idling is dangerous. On the surface, you look active, you're in meetings, and replying to emails. But inside, your mind is dull, you're thinking mechanical, your attention scattered. You're not driving anything. You're coasting.

This is where innovation dies. Creativity disappears. Emotional intelligence fades. And leadership becomes robotic.

Breaking the Idle Loop

So, how do you stay out of the idle loop?

For me, it starts with a very simple principle: Begin your day with energy.

For the last 25 years, I've followed a morning ritual. I wake up around 5 AM and begin my fitness routine, anywhere between 60 and 90 minutes. Some days it's intense, some days it's light stretching or a walk. But I never skip it.

This is not about fitness goals. It's about energy goals.

When I exercise in the morning, I feel switched on, physically, mentally, and emotionally. My body is alive, my mind is alert, and my mood is elevated. It creates a ripple effect that carries into everything I do.

Immediately after that, I spend 30 quiet minutes planning my day. I think about what's ahead, what kind of energy each part of the day will need. I plan my meals, my coffee breaks, and even my low-energy recovery moments.

Yes, planning your coffee is also planning your energy. Anticipation itself creates energy. When your brain knows a treat or reward is coming, it sends a signal to perk up.

Before my meetings, I write 2–3 lines in a notebook about what I think might happen. It's not a prediction. It's more like a mental warm-up, a way of priming my attention. When the meeting starts, I'm already engaged. I'm looking for clues. I'm tuned in.

That's the opposite of idling.

Recognizing and Managing Your Dips

Of course, not all meetings are energizing. Some are repetitive. Some are draining. Some feel like a slow slide into mental fog.

You need to plan for those, too.

For example, when I attend conferences, I know the first hour or two will be exciting: keynotes, networking, new ideas. But after that, there's a dip. Endless presentations, overcrowded booths, and tired conversations.

I don't fight the dip. I plan around it.

I schedule breaks. I walk over to meet a vendor I'm curious about. I step outside for air. I chat with someone random. That break in monotony helps me reset and return with attention.

Some days, despite my best planning, I hit a wall. The fatigue is real. My rituals don't work. That's when I shift strategy. I call a friend. Crack a joke. Watch a movie clip. Do something silly or spontaneous.

That randomness brings unexpected energy. It's the opposite of the structured morning, and yet, equally powerful. It reminds me I'm not a machine. I'm human. And humans can refresh through connection, laughter, and unpredictability.

Energy Is Your Leadership Fuel

What powers a leader?

It's not just knowledge. It's not just confidence or clarity. It's energy, your internal fuel that drives every decision, every interaction, every moment of influence.

We often think of energy as something passive, something we "have" or "lack." But energy is much more than a feeling. It is a tactical resource to which leaders need to provide management. Leaders need to make time to watch their mental, emotional, and physical energy, just like professional athletes count their calories and water intake, if they are to continue performing, influencing others, and staying creative despite the pressure.

Nonetheless, we all spend our days oblivious to energy fluctuations. We do not trace it. We do not organize it. And that is why we get so tired, grumpy, uninspired, or distracted at mid-afternoon.

As a matter of fact, energy is not unlimited but is renewable, provided that you know how to make use of it.

The Two Boxes: How Your Brain Categorizes Tasks

Let's start with how our brain processes activities.

Everything we do gets subconsciously sorted into two categories:

1. The "Happy Box"

These are the tasks and experiences that give you energy, the moments when you're in flow. This box includes:

- Organic activities that are your inner strengths.
- The things you like doing: listening to music, designing something, having a deep conversation, playing sports, solving puzzles, and teaching.
- Communication that makes you happy, that is funny, or that helps you feel that something bigger was accomplished.

When you're operating from the Happy Box, time flies. Your mind is sharp. Your motivation is intrinsic. You feel "lit up" inside, not because someone is pushing you, but because something within you is pulling you.

2. The "Duty Box"

This is where most of our adult lives happen. The Duty Box includes:

- Tasks we don't necessarily enjoy but must do, like meetings, financial reports, performance reviews, logistics planning, or documentation.
- Responsibilities that may be important but don't energize us.

The Duty Box isn't bad. It's necessary. But if we operate out of it for too long without replenishment, we start to drain. The brain experiences these tasks as energy outflow without emotional return.

When your whole day sits in the Duty Box, it becomes a slow leak of vitality.

The Danger Zone: When You Enter "Idle" Mode

So what happens when both boxes are neglected or mismanaged?

You slide into the Idle Zone, the most dangerous mental state for any leader.

Idle mode looks like:

- Sitting through meetings without really listening.
- Skimming emails while multitasking.

- Saying “yes” to things by default.
- Feeling fatigued even after rest.
- Delaying decisions or procrastinating without clarity on why.

In idle mode, your brain is conserving energy, not engaging. It’s not resting, but it’s also not creating. It's drifting, passively consuming instead of actively contributing.

This is where innovation dies.

This is where your decision-making slows down, your conversations become shallow, and your team feels the disconnection. Because energy isn't just internal, it’s visible. People around you can tell when your spark is gone.

In fact, charisma, that magnetic presence we associate with leaders, is simply well-managed energy made visible.

Energy vs Time: A Better Metric

We’ve all heard it: “Time is your most valuable resource.”

But that’s only half true. The real resource is how much energy you have for the time you’re given.

You can block out three hours to work on a strategy, but if your energy is low, those three hours will produce ten minutes of value. On the flip side, if you’re fully engaged, you can create impact in twenty minutes that others might take hours to achieve.

That's why great leaders don't just manage time. They manage energy rhythms.

They ask:

- When during the day am I most alert, creative, and focused?
- Which people or tasks lift me up?
- What routines help me reset?

When you begin to prioritize energy zones over time slots, your output and satisfaction both multiply.

How Energy Loss Impacts Leadership

Let's go deeper. What actually happens when your energy declines, not just physically, but mentally and emotionally?

1. Poor Decision-Making

When your brain is tired, it defaults to the familiar. You avoid risk, ignore nuance, and choose the easiest available option. This isn't always a disaster, but over time, it leads to mediocrity.

In low-energy states, we make decisions to end discomfort, not to maximize opportunity.

2. Reduced Clarity and Vision

Energy affects perspective. When you are exhausted, you concentrate on fires of the day rather than creating a long-term impression. The strategic lens becomes narrow, and you do not see the woods and trees.

That is why weary leaders become reactive leaders, able to deal with symptoms but unable to address underlying problems.

3. Loss of Charisma

People don't follow knowledge. They follow aliveness. A drained leader may still be technically correct, but their communication lacks conviction. Their presence doesn't uplift the room. Their tone feels heavy. Teams feel that.

A tired leader can still lead tasks. But they can't inspire people.

Tracking Your Energy: Awareness Creates Power

One of the most powerful habits I've built is tracking my energy across a typical week. It's simple, but transformative.

Here's how you can do it:

The Energy Tracker Tool

Create a table with each day of the week as columns and the following time slots as rows:

- Early morning (6 AM – 9 AM)
- Late morning (9 AM – 12 PM)

- Afternoon (12 PM – 3 PM)
- Late afternoon (3 PM – 6 PM)
- Evening (6 PM – 9 PM)

Each time block, rate your energy on a scale of 1 to 5:

- 1 = Depleted, foggy, passive
- 3 = Average, functional, okay
- 5 = High energy, clear, engaged

Do this for 5 days. At the end of the week, review the pattern.

Ask yourself:

- What were my top-performing hours?
- What consistently drained me?
- Which people or activities show up around high or low moments?
- How can I redesign my schedule to match my natural rhythm?

Once you map your energy profile, you stop working against yourself. You start aligning your work with your power windows.

Practical Redesigns: Small Shifts, Big Returns

You don't need to overhaul your life. Start with small experiments. For example:

- Move creative work (strategy, writing, problem-solving) to your highest energy window.
- Group admin tasks into low-energy slots where they won't feel overwhelming.
- Block recovery buffers after energy-depleting tasks or meetings.
- Insert joy triggers during the day: walk breaks, quick playlists, humor breaks, a 10-minute call with someone energizing.

These are not time wasters. They're voltage boosters. The more often you charge, the longer your performance lasts.

A Word on Emotional Energy

While we talk a lot about physical and mental energy, emotional energy is just as critical. And often, more fragile.

Here's what drains emotional energy:

- Unresolved conflict
- Poor communication
- Feeling unappreciated
- Carrying guilt or perfectionism
- Inauthenticity (pretending to care when you don't)

Here's what restores it:

- Meaningful conversations
- Acts of kindness
- Celebrating small wins
- Humor, gratitude, storytelling
- Being fully yourself, even if it's imperfect

If you're emotionally tired, don't just take a nap. Talk. Laugh. Express. Forgive. Be human.

Because leadership isn't robotic. It's relational. And that means your emotional battery is the most visible to others, and the most contagious.

Energy Is a Choice, Not Just a Condition

One of the most empowering realizations I've had is this: Energy is not random. It's responsive.

It responds to the environment.

It responds to meaning.

It responds to rhythm.

It responds to how well you know yourself.

When you make energy a priority, everything else improves: your thinking, your communication, your leadership.

Because people don't just follow your ideas. They follow your energy.

Discipline as the Engine

Everyone wants to feel energized. Everyone wants to lead with confidence and clarity. But very few are willing to build the system that makes it possible every single day. That system is called discipline.

Discipline isn't sexy. It doesn't trend on social media. It doesn't get applause in meetings. But it's the most powerful engine behind any successful, consistent leader I've ever known. You may not see it, but it's there, quietly holding the whole operation together.

It's not about being perfect. It's about showing up, especially when you don't feel like it.

I've been waking up at 5 AM for the last 25 years. Not because I'm some ultra-disciplined superhero. But because I realized early on that the most valuable energy I have is in the first few hours of my day. If I don't use it intentionally, I lose it to chaos.

Some mornings, my body doesn't want to move. Some mornings, my mind is foggy, and the idea of going through the motions feels pointless. But I still get up. I still move. Sometimes it's an intense workout. Sometimes it's just walking, stretching, breathing. The level changes. The ritual doesn't.

That's discipline.

And here's the secret: It's not restrictive. It's freeing.

Discipline Creates Freedom

There's a myth that discipline limits spontaneity. That it boxes you in. But in reality, discipline is what creates space for spontaneity, creativity, and joy. Why? Because when your mind isn't constantly firefighting, wondering what to do next, stressing over deadlines, reacting to problems, you have margin. You have clarity. You have room to think, feel, and create.

Imagine your life like a power plant. If you let energy leak all day, through distractions, poor planning, endless scrolling, and reactive decisions, then by midday, you're drained. You're now depending on stimulants, motivation videos, or adrenaline to push through. But if you manage your energy early, with structure and rhythm, you last longer, stronger, and smarter.

Discipline isn't just about the body. It's about your time, your focus, and your emotional space.

One of the most impactful changes I made was learning to plan my day with intention. After my morning workout, I spend 30 minutes in stillness. I look at my calendar, review my commitments, and identify the meetings or activities that will demand the most of me. I visualize how I want to show up.

Then I plan something simple but strategic: my food and break schedule.

I know it sounds mundane, but it's actually deeply psychological. When your mind knows a snack, a coffee, or a pause is coming at a specific time, it relaxes. Anticipation becomes energy. Instead of wondering when you'll get a breather, your brain paces itself toward that milestone.

Even toddlers understand this. You tell a child, "After you finish cleaning, we'll go to the park," and suddenly they have purpose. We don't lose that need as adults; we just forget how to structure it.

Mini-Habits, Maximum Impact

Discipline doesn't have to be overwhelming. You don't need a 50-step productivity system or a color-coded life calendar. What you need are mini-habits that anchor you.

Here are three habits that transformed my energy game:

1. The Energy Pulse Check

At least once every two hours, I pause and ask myself: "Where is my energy right now?" Am I buzzing with clarity? Am I dragging? Am I drifting into autopilot?

If I'm on a high, I double down. I knock off high-effort tasks. I make key decisions. If I'm low, I don't force it. I step away, walk, breathe, chat with someone, or switch tasks for a mental reset.

This habit trains you to manage energy, not just time.

2. Meeting Priming

Before every important meeting, I write 2–3 lines in a small notebook about what I anticipate might happen. Not expectations, just anticipations.

This mental rehearsal does two things:

- It creates focus and alertness. I walk into the meeting, tuned in.
- It builds curiosity; I want to see how the event unfolds compared to what I imagined.

Suddenly, even a dry or difficult meeting becomes an intellectual game. You're no longer passively sitting through it. You're actively observing, engaging, and noticing patterns.

3. End-of-Day Check-in

At the end of each day, I write a sentence or two:

- What energized me today?
- What drained me?

- What do I want to do differently tomorrow?

This takes 3 minutes. But over a week, it gives you a pattern map of your energy. You begin to see trends, who, what, when, and where your energy shifts. Self-awareness is the foundation of self-leadership.

Dealing with Discipline Fatigue

But let's be real. Even the most disciplined routines face resistance. You'll have days when nothing goes to plan. Days when your rituals feel flat. Days when your body is tired and your mind is uninspired.

What do you do then?

The key is grace, not guilt.

I used to beat myself up on days when I missed a workout or let my energy crash. Now, I treat those days as signal days. They tell me something. Maybe I've been pushing too hard. Maybe I need rest, not another productivity hack. Maybe I need connection, a friend, a laugh, a good story.

Sometimes the best way to regain discipline is to step away from it briefly, to return with intention, not obligation.

Discipline isn't a punishment. It's a partnership between your vision and your values. If the rhythm breaks, you don't quit the song. You just find your beat again.

Structure Beats Willpower

Here's another truth I learned the hard way: Willpower is overrated. Structure is underrated.

Most people rely on willpower to get through the day:

- "I'll try to eat healthy."
- "I'll do my best to focus."
- "I'll exercise if I find time."

That's a recipe for inconsistency. Because willpower is finite. It depletes with every decision, every stressor, every distraction.

Structure, on the other hand, is automatic. When something is part of your default setting, it takes less mental energy to do it. You don't wake up wondering whether to brush your teeth. You just do it.

What if your morning workout, your energy breaks, your gratitude journaling, your evening reset, what if all of these were part of your "brush your teeth" routine?

That's what structure does. It removes friction. And friction is the enemy of consistency.

Creating Your Personal Energy Operating System

Think of yourself as a high-performance athlete. You don't just show up on race day and hope for the best. You train. You recover. You manage your cycles. You have a system.

Leadership is the same. If you want to lead with power, you need a personal operating system that protects and fuels your energy.

Here are five questions to help you build that system:

1. What's your peak energy window each day?
    - Morning? Late night? Midday?
    - Schedule your highest-value work in that window.
2. What drains you the fastest?
    - Certain people, meetings, environments?
    - Can you minimize or redesign those experiences?
3. What rituals ground you?
    - Morning workouts, journaling, prayer, walks?
    - Build them into your core schedule, not the leftovers.
4. What does "rest" mean for you?
    - Is it solitude? Nature? Music? Laughter?
    - Use rest strategically, not reactively.
5. When do you lose rhythm?
    - After travel? After tough feedback? After success?

- Create pre-set recovery protocols for those moments.

Your energy is too precious to leave to chance. It deserves a system.

Discipline Is the Silent Leader

You may never get an award for discipline. No one may clap when you wake up early, stretch instead of scroll, or pause instead of push. But that quiet consistency is what sets the real leaders apart.

Discipline is not about being rigid. It's about being ready. Ready to rise. Ready to serve. Ready to adapt.

And when others see you consistently showing up with energy, calm, and clarity, they won't just follow you. They'll trust you.

Because energy is contagious. But so is exhaustion. And leaders set the tone.

Strategically Managing Low-Energy Zones

Even the most disciplined, self-aware leaders hit a wall sometimes. You can wake up early, exercise, journal, plan your meals, and still find yourself at 3:30 PM in a windowless conference room, stuck in what I call "energy death."

It's not burnout. It's not laziness. It's just natural rhythm; the human body and brain were never designed for endless output.

Recognizing and managing this rhythm isn't a weakness. It's wisdom.

If energy is your leadership fuel, then knowing when your tank hits empty and how to refill it is a crucial survival skill. In fact, the most effective leaders I've worked with were not the ones who never tired, but the ones who could strategically recover and redirect when they did.

Let's talk about how.

Recognize Your Personal Energy Rhythm

Every one of us has a unique energy blueprint. It's the natural rise and fall of your focus, enthusiasm, and mental sharpness across a typical day or week.

For example, I've discovered:

- My high-performance window is between 5 AM and 9 AM. That's when I tackle strategy, writing, tough decisions, or anything that needs deep thinking.
- My first dip happens around 11:30 AM, just before lunch.
- Post-lunch hours (2–3:30 PM) are the danger zone, where idling and distraction are most likely.

- Energy tends to rebound around 4–5 PM, especially if I've taken a short reset break.

Once you start mapping this for yourself, you gain clarity.

Ask yourself:

- When do I feel naturally focused?
- When do I tend to procrastinate?
- Which meetings or tasks drain me most?
- What kind of work do I do best in each part of the day?

This awareness is powerful. Because most people blame themselves during energy dips. They assume they're weak, lazy, or unmotivated. But in reality, they're just human.

And once you accept that dips are inevitable, you stop fighting them and start planning around them.

The Usual Suspects: Meetings, Conferences & Online Classes

Let's address some of the most notorious energy-killers in modern professional life.

1. Back-to-back Meetings

Meetings without pause are like running a marathon with no water. By the third or fourth meeting, your attention shrinks, your listening drops, and your presence fades.

But here's the trick: It's not the number of meetings that hurts you; it's the lack of recovery between them.

Build intentional gaps. Even five minutes to stretch, breathe, or simply reset your eyes can dramatically improve energy carryover.

2. Long Conferences

There's a unique kind of fatigue that sets in after the first few hours of a day-long conference. You're surrounded by information, movement, and people, but slowly, your brain checks out.

I call this the "death by PowerPoint" syndrome.

I've sat through full-day conferences that were technically excellent, yet deeply exhausting. Endless slides. Predictable content. Monotonous delivery.

Eventually, no matter how sharp the speaker is, the brain resists more input.

3. Online Classes or Webinars

Remote fatigue is real. The lack of movement, small screen size, and limited interaction lead to cognitive drain. The brain works harder to interpret visual cues, fill in emotional gaps, and stay attentive.

Here's what I've learned: You can't always escape these situations, but you can design your way through them.

<u>Anecdote: How I Survived "Death by PowerPoint"</u>

Let me share a story.

A few years ago, I was at a high-profile leadership summit overseas. The event was over three days, and while the opening sessions were inspiring, by the afternoon of Day 1, things started to blur.

Slide after slide. Buzzwords. Case studies that all started sounding the same. People around me were discreetly checking phones, sipping coffee for the third time, or sneaking out.

I could feel myself slipping into mental hibernation.

Instead of powering through, I paused. I looked at the agenda and quickly mapped out:

- Which sessions felt repetitive?
- Which speakers or vendors intrigued me?
- When could I take a purposeful break without missing something crucial?

Here's what I did:

- During low-interest segments, I stepped outside and struck up conversations with vendors or attendees I had marked as potential collaborators.

- I scheduled walk breaks every 90 minutes, even if it was just around the venue.
- I used one session break to write down three insights from the morning, actively consolidating my learning so my brain could "close a loop" before opening a new one.

The result? I stayed engaged, met fascinating people, and actually remembered more than I usually do at such events.

The lesson: Don't just attend. Intentionally design your participation.

Energy Interjections: The Science of Resetting Your Brain

When you're stuck in a low-energy state, you need what I call energy interjections, brief, intentional disruptions that re-activate your nervous system and increase dopamine, oxygen, or social connection.

Here are a few powerful interjections you can apply:

1. Physical Shift

Stand up. Stretch. Walk around. Change posture. Movement increases blood flow to the brain and helps reset attention.

Even small shifts, like standing during a call or stepping outside for 3 minutes, have a massive effect.

2. Light Socializing

Humans are social animals. A casual connection can recharge you faster than isolation. Chat with a colleague. Tell a joke. Ask a question. Share a moment of vulnerability or humor.

It signals to your brain: "I'm not alone in this. I'm safe. I can re-engage."

3. Humor

Humor is a biological reset button. It activates multiple regions of the brain, reduces cortisol (the stress hormone), and increases emotional bonding.

During a tough afternoon meeting, I often throw in a light comment or tell a story that breaks the tension. The smiles that follow aren't just polite, they're physiological releases. They wake the room up.

4. Environmental Tweaks

Change your settings. Open a window. Shift the lighting. Adjust the temperature. Your surroundings constantly influence your cognitive performance.

Even rearranging your desktop items or switching your screen background can refresh your visual field.

Tool: Micro-Strategy for Low-Energy Events

Here's a simple 5-step micro-strategy you can apply before any event or meeting you suspect will be energy-draining.

1. Predict the Dip

Ask:

- When during the event do I usually start to zone out?
- What kind of content/format usually triggers fatigue?

2. Set Anchors

Pick one or two elements to stay engaged:

- A person you want to meet or observe
- A concept you're curious to learn
- A question you want answered

Anchors help you retain purpose even when interest wanes.

3. Plan Breaks Ahead

Look for windows to pause. Even a 5-minute breather outside the meeting room can make a difference.

If breaks aren't scheduled, create micro-pauses:

- Take notes during slow moments.

- Doodle or draw concepts you hear.
- Engage your brain in subtle movement.

4. Prime Your Body

Before the event starts, energize your body:

- Hydrate.
- Take a brisk walk.
- Do 10 squats or light stretches.

Pre-loading the body with oxygen and movement delays the onset of cognitive fatigue.

5. Use the Power of Debrief

Afterward, consolidate your learning.

- Write 3 takeaways.
- Reflect on what drained or energized you.
- Decide how you'll do it differently next time.

Every event becomes a training ground for your energy intelligence.

Building Your Daily Power Ritual

The quality of your day is rarely determined by what happens to you. It's determined by how you show up to meet it. And how you show up is defined, more than anything, by the first hour of your day.

That's why world-class leaders, athletes, and creatives all talk about the same thing: the power of the morning ritual.

It's not about being a "morning person." It's about having a system that tunes your body, mind, and spirit into a state of readiness. A state of ignition.

I call this the Morning Power Ritual, a 3-part, 20–45-minute routine that activates your full self before the world demands a piece of you.

Let's break it down.

The Morning Power Ritual: 3 Parts to Activate You

1. Physical Activation – Wake the Body, Unlock the Mind

Your body is the foundation of your energy. When it moves, your brain lights up. When you're stiff, so is your thinking. When you sweat, stretch, or breathe deeply, your nervous system shifts gears.

That's why the first step in the ritual is movement.

You don't need an intense 90-minute gym session. You need consistent activation.

Options:

- A 15-minute bodyweight workout
- 10 sun salutations or yoga poses
- A 20-minute brisk walk or light jog
- Breathwork or dynamic stretching
- Dancing to your favorite playlist

The goal isn't to burn calories. It's to send a clear signal to your brain: I'm awake, I'm here, I'm ready.

Even 5–10 minutes of mindful movement oxygenates the brain, sharpens focus, and lifts your emotional state.

On days when you're short on time, even standing with your arms raised and taking 10 deep breaths can activate your posture and mindset.

Remember: Energy isn't created by thought. It's triggered by movement.

2. Mental Planning – Design Your Day with Intention

Once your body is activated, your mind is awake. This is when most people rush to check messages, headlines, or emails, all of which put you into reactive mode.

The alternative? Pause and plan. Lead your day before it leads you.

Spend 10–15 minutes in intentional mental framing. This includes:

- Reviewing your calendar or to-do list
- Visualizing your top 3 priorities
- Anticipating moments where energy might dip
- Choosing your tone: calm, focused, patient, assertive?

A helpful exercise:
Write down three meetings or events and one sentence about what you anticipate from each.

This act of pre-framing improves attention, helps you stay mentally present, and reduces decision fatigue.

You don't need a fancy planner. Just a notebook, digital app, or calendar will do. What matters is ownership; you are no longer just responding. You are directing.

This part of the ritual trains your brain to see your day before it happens, and that creates clarity.

3. Emotional Priming – Set Your Inner Vibe

The last piece is often the most overlooked, but possibly the most powerful. It's the part that sets your emotional frequency for the day.

I call it emotional priming, a 5–10-minute practice that calibrates your internal state.

There are two ways to do this:

A. Anticipation Journaling

Write 2–3 lines about something you look forward to that day. It could be:

- A conversation
- A project milestone
- A moment of solitude
- A coffee with someone
- A break where you'll listen to music

Anticipation creates energy. The brain rewards anticipation with dopamine. You now walk into your day with a sense of positive expectancy.

B. Gratitude Logging

Write 3 things you're grateful for. They can be simple:

- "The silence of the morning"
- "My partner's support"

- "The strength in my legs today"

Gratitude doesn't erase problems. It gives you a lens to see possibilities, not just pressures.

This part is deeply emotional. You'll be surprised how a small entry in a journal can recalibrate your entire nervous system.

Start your day in a positive emotional state, and you build resilience for whatever challenge comes.

<u>Putting It All Together: A Sample Morning Power Ritual (30 minutes)</u>

Time	Activity
5:30–5:45 AM	Physical activation (yoga + pushups)
5:45–6:00 AM	Calendar review + write anticipation notes
6:00–6:10 AM	Gratitude journaling + breathwork
6:10 AM onward	Begin work with a focused, high-energy mindset

This structure is fluid. Some days it's 15 minutes. Other days it's 45. What matters is consistency over perfection.

Your Grit Score: Measuring Discipline Over Time

If energy is the engine, grit is the oil that keeps it running over time.

Grit is not about being intense for one day. It's about being consistent for weeks, even when motivation fades. Especially when no one is watching.

To assess your Personal Grit Score, reflect on the last 7 days:

Prompt	Response (0–5)
How consistently did I follow my morning routine?	
Did I show up for my workout, even when I didn't feel like it?	
Did I plan my day rather than just react?	
How well did I manage energy dips without disengaging?	

Did I choose growth habits over comfort?	
Did I reset quickly after off-days?	

Total Score: /30

- 25–30: High Grit – You're building elite-level consistency.
- 18–24: Good Progress – A few tweaks away from peak performance.
- 10–17: Awareness Stage – You know what to do, now commit.
- <10: Reboot Needed – Time to simplify and restart.

Use this self-assessment weekly or monthly to recalibrate. Track your score. Watch how grit compounds your energy.

Tools You Can Use: Templates & Trackers

Here are three tools to help you operationalize what you've learned:

1. Morning Power Ritual Planner

A simple one-pager with these sections:

- Movement (checklist or log)
- Mental framing (top 3 priorities, schedule scan)

- Emotional priming (anticipation + gratitude)

Use daily for 21 days to build the habit.

2. Energy Tracker Template

Track your energy in 3-hour blocks each day:

- Rate from 1–5
- Note task/context
- Observe patterns

Use weekly to redesign your work rhythm.

3. Grit Score Journal Page

Copy the Grit Score table and reflect on each week. Write 2 lines on:

- Where you did well
- Where do you need to re-anchor

Small reflections lead to sustained behavior change.

The One Change You'll Commit to for 21 Days

Now that you understand your energy, your rhythm, and your internal levers, it's time to choose one ritual to commit to.

Not ten. Just one.

Ask yourself:

- Which part of the Morning Power Ritual zo I need the most right now, physical, mental, or emotional?
- What's one small change I can start tomorrow?
- What will I do when I miss a day?
- How will I reset with grace?
- Who can I share this commitment with for accountability?

Write it down. Say it aloud. Track it for 21 days. That's how momentum begins.

Because in the end, power doesn't come from intensity. It comes from identity.

You are someone who shows up, even when it's inconvenient. Especially then.

And when your morning starts with power, so does your leadership.

Chapter 2: Hard Work is Not the Hero

The Hustle Illusion – Why Hard Work Doesn't Equal Success

It is pleasing to know that one day this hard work will pay off. It leads us to be on the illusion of being in control: If I put in a shift, then I will work longer, do more, and then success will be the icing on the cake. It's an attractive notion. But it's a dangerous illusion. Because the reality is, effort without direction is nothing but motion without progress.

During my experience in the management of high-performing teams over the years, I have witnessed the hustle culture myth replay and play. Departments that never sleep, where people work late into the night, skip weekends, and answer midnight emails. It may seem cool on the external, but it can mean that something is wrong on the internal: strategic misalignment.

Hard work is nice. There's a sense of the rush of dopamine in checking something off, the pride that comes with coming in late. But the question is, are we getting closer to the goal, or are we going in circles?

Let me begin with a straightforward fact: not all hard work is the same.

Think about the metaphor of a runner on a treadmill. You can be running flat out, sweat dripping, heart pounding. But if you're not actually going somewhere, what's it for? Now imagine that, compared to someone walking quickly outside, stepping purposefully towards a familiar endpoint. Who's actually getting anywhere?

Imagine two people trying to cross a river.

One grabs a shovel and starts digging — working non-stop, sweating, dirt flying everywhere. He believes that if he just digs deep enough, maybe he'll tunnel under the river. He's working incredibly hard.

The other steps back, studies the landscape, and starts assembling a simple wooden bridge. Slower at first, but every plank takes her closer to the other side.

By the end of the day, one has a deep, muddy pit. The other is already walking across.

Moral: Digging harder won't get you across the river. Building smarter will.

That's the essence of smart work: it's not about pace or endurance, it's about direction.

The Emotional High of Being Busy

One of the biggest addictive pieces of hustle culture is that it feels so emotionally rewarding. Being busy makes us feel important. It makes us feel needed. When we're working late, we say to ourselves that we're doing more. When our schedules are full, we feel essential. We confuse fullness with value.

But here's the irony: busyness tends to replace effectiveness.

When you're going from task to task in a rush, there's no room to think, to think through, to course-correct. You're an output machine, not an outcomes driver.

I've been in so many reviews with teams that gleefully show off how much time they put in, how much code they wrote, how many customer tickets they resolved. And my same old follow-up question is: What difference did that make?

You can get a hundred things right and still get that one thing wrong that counts.

The Pitfall of Misdirected Discipline

Hustle culture schools us on the idea that grit is the highest virtue. Giving up is a weakness. That slowing down is laziness. But true discipline isn't merely about persevering; it's about understanding when to hold back and reconsider.

Take sports, for instance. Athletes do not train continuously. They train with intensity, then recover with intensity. Muscle is a product of rest, not the gym. Overtraining will not make you stronger; it will break you down.

Why should the workplace be any different?

Working without recovery, emotionally or mentally, results in burnout, errors, and disillusionment. Actual performance comes from sustainable intensity, not perpetual grind.

We must instruct teams that astute leaders are able to pull back, zoom out, and simply ask: Is this still in the right direction?

Story: The Internship Wake-up Call

I recall my first significant internship project. I was green, hungry, and dead set on demonstrating my capabilities. The project was to develop an exhaustive market analysis of a new product category. I dove headfirst into the task, reading, researching, and filling out data late into the night.

After two weeks, I had this enormous report, more than 70 pages. I was so proud. I felt I had labored more than anyone else. But when I showed it to my manager, he flipped through some pages, then asked, "What are the top three insights?"

I was shocked. I had information, not insights. Bulk, not wisdom. He explained to me kindly, "This is a good effort, but it's not actionable. I need you to go back, and this time, give me five pages, just the things I need to make a decision."

That lesson stuck with me forever: hard work is not sufficient. You must work towards the right result.

From Effort to Effectiveness

Let's clarify one thing: this is not a criticism of hard work. Effort is essential. But the effort must be pointed. It must be in service of something greater than itself.

Too often, teams equate effort with effectiveness:

- "We spent 1000 hours building this."
- "We stayed up all night to finish it."
- "We deployed on time, no matter what."

But without linking those statements to business impact, they become hollow.

Smart work asks:

- Did we solve the real problem?
- Did we move the needle on the metric that matters?
- Did we design this around the end-user, not just our internal timeline?

When Leaders Enable the Hustle Trap

As leaders, we often unintentionally reinforce hustle culture. We reward the people who stay late. We praise the ones who take on more. We overlook those who work quietly, efficiently, and go home on time. Why?

Because we've been conditioned to equate visibility with value.

But some of the most impactful contributors are not loud. They're strategic. They cut through the noise. They do the few things that truly matter.

We need to shift the narrative. Instead of asking, “Who’s working hardest?” ask, “Who’s driving the most value?”

The Trap of Tasks

It’s easy to get caught in the trap of tasks. You start the day with a checklist. You finish it with all items checked. That feels great. But did any of those tasks truly matter?

There’s a difference between progress and motion. Between being busy and being effective.

You can fill your day with emails, meetings, reports, and updates. But if none of that contributes to a meaningful outcome, you’ve simply spent energy, not invested it.

True productivity is not about doing more. It’s about doing less of the unimportant and more of the impactful.

Take a few moments to consider:

- What are the top 3 things you did last week?
- Did they contribute directly to a key outcome or just help you stay afloat?
- If you stopped doing 20% of your tasks, would anything break? Or would you just feel less "busy"?

These questions are not about guilt. They’re about growth.

Tool: Excellence vs. Perfection Grid

To help distinguish meaningful effort from wasted motion, try this simple decision grid:

	Low Value Outcome	High Value Outcome
Low Effort	Ignore	Automate/Delegate
High Effort	Stop/Question	Invest Deeply

Before diving into a task, ask:

- What's the potential outcome?
- How much effort will it take?
- Is it worth it?

Sometimes, the smart move is not to push harder, but to step back and reframe the approach.

From Activity to Impact – Rethinking the Workday

We like to feel productive.

There's something satisfying about checking off a task list, about crossing out line after line in a journal, or seeing a full calendar. It gives us the illusion of movement. Of value. Of progress.

But here's the truth: Movement is not progress.

And in leadership, movement without direction can be the costliest mistake.

I've seen this firsthand.

The Illusion of Progress

We were nearing the end of a major product development cycle, six months in the making. Teams had worked hard. Really hard. Product management, engineering, testing, documentation, and customer support, everyone was dialed in. Status meetings were optimistic. Metrics showed green lights across the board. The release was on time, perhaps even a little early.

On paper, we were winning.

But something bothered me. The excitement felt too self-contained. Too... internal.

That's when I asked a seemingly innocent question in a leadership meeting:

"How will this product release impact our top five customers?"

There was silence for a moment. Then, a few hopeful answers, mentions of certain features, customer feedback quotes, and some market positioning language.

But none of it was sharp. None of it was specific.

So I pushed further.

"Do we know exactly how this will drive revenue, either from existing clients or from new acquisitions?"

That's when things started to unravel.

We realized we hadn't aligned feature prioritization with revenue potential. Instead, many decisions had been made based on resource availability, what could be done, rather than what should be done.

A few days later, when we regrouped, the picture was clearer and more concerning. The features most valuable to our biggest clients had been deprioritized because they were complex, required architectural changes, or needed additional testing.

Meanwhile, smaller features with easier delivery paths had taken priority.

It wasn't because people didn't care. It was because we had defaulted to task thinking. We had fallen into a trap that most teams and most leaders fall into at some point:

Optimizing for output instead of outcome.

Inside-Out vs. Outside-In Thinking

The core problem here was inside-out planning.

We were looking at:

- What the team was capable of delivering.
- What resources were available?
- What could fit into the timeline?

All of that matters. But none of that automatically means value to the customer or value to the business.

Outside-in thinking flips the lens:

- What does the customer need the most?
- What will change their experience or ROI?
  What will impact our competitive position or revenue?

When teams plan inside-out, they often end up shipping effort instead of shipping impact.

That's what was happening in our product release. We were releasing something. But not necessarily the right thing.

Smart Work ≠ Easy Work

Now, let me clarify something.

Smart work is not a shortcut. It's not about avoiding hard tasks or doing less. In fact, smart work often involves more discomfort. More confrontation with trade-offs. More pausing to reflect, challenge assumptions, and reset.

But it leads to greater clarity and leverage.

In our case, we had a decision to make.

Do we launch the product as scheduled, fully aware that our top customers might be underwhelmed?

Or do we stall the release, revisit the roadmap, and prioritize the three features that truly moved the needle?

It wasn't an easy call.

The teams had already invested deeply. Morale was tied to the release. Momentum was high. But in leadership, sometimes your role is to protect the mission, not the momentum.

I chose to delay.

Yes, it created temporary frustration. But it also gave us a second chance to align execution with strategy.

We shipped a refined version a few weeks later. And this time, the release was met with immediate adoption by our top clients. Our credibility increased, not decreased. And the revenue impact was measurable.

That's what smart work looks like in action.

Activity vs. Impact: Knowing the Difference

So, how do we prevent these traps?

It starts with developing a mental habit, asking, "Is this activity creating real impact?"

Here's a simple filter I use when reviewing tasks, meetings, or roadmaps:

Activity	Question to Ask	Smart Response
New feature or project	Who benefits the most? Will this change behavior, revenue, or satisfaction?	Align priorities with outcomes, not effort
Status meetings	What decisions are being made from this data?	Shift from reporting to insight sharing
Team workloads	Are we maximizing effort or maximizing leverage?	Focus on high-leverage contributions
Email responses or presentations	Is this needed, or just expected?	Trim the excess; automate where possible

Smart work is not lazy. It's focused.

It's saying no to ten things so you can say yes to the one that changes the game.

Why Smart Work Feels Uncomfortable

The reason many people default to working hard rather than working smart is that smart work requires uncomfortable truths:

- That not all effort is equal.
- That some of what we're doing might be wasted.
- That being busy doesn't always mean being valuable.

It also requires something even scarier: letting go of effort that makes us feel good but doesn't deliver results.

In fact, many people attach their identity to hard work.

They say things like:

- "I stayed up all night working on this."
- "We've been working on this for six months straight."
- "I skipped my vacation to get this out."

These are acts of dedication, and they should be respected.

But they are not metrics of success.

The smarter question is: "What impact did your work have?"

That's where great leadership lies, in separating effort from outcome.

Redesigning Your Workday: The Smart Work Canvas

One of the simplest tools I share with teams is the Smart Work Canvas, a weekly check-in tool that helps redesign your calendar and focus.

Here's how it works:

Step 1: Map Your Week

Take your previous week and divide your time into blocks of:

- High-effort, low-impact
- High-effort, high-impact
- Low-effort, low-impact
- Low-effort, high-impact

Step 2: Reflect and Reassign

For each block:

- Eliminate or automate low-impact work
- Invest in expanding high-impact zones
- Delegate what someone else could do 80% as well
- Re-prioritize tasks based on business goals

This visual reset helps shift from task addiction to value creation.

Once you see your week laid out, patterns emerge:

- Maybe you're spending too much time in meetings that don't result in decisions.
- Maybe your best creative window is wasted on email.
- Maybe you're doing work that doesn't match your title or your potential.

Smart work means realigning time with purpose, not just productivity.

Leadership's Role in Refocusing Effort

Leaders have a unique role in guiding this transition. You don't just manage projects; you shape how people spend their energy.

Here's how you lead smarter work:

1. Ask "Why" Often – Challenge the automatic habits.
2. Model It – Stop glorifying long hours. Celebrate insight, clarity, and courage to change.
3. Reward Value, Not Volume – Make room for innovation by reducing unnecessary grind.
4. Schedule White Space – Give your team space to think, not just do.
5. Protect the Mission – If execution is drifting from strategy, pause. Reset. Realign.

A Leadership Mindset Shift: From Effort to Influence

Ultimately, the shift from hard work to smart work is a mindset evolution.

You begin to realize:

- That your role isn't to do everything, but to do what matters.
- Real leadership isn't about pushing people to work harder, but guiding them to work wiser.
- That slowing down sometimes creates the biggest breakthroughs.

The day I chose to pause our product release wasn't because the team wasn't working hard. It was because they were, and that effort deserved to matter.

Leadership is about protecting that effort from being wasted on the wrong outcome.

Think about your current week:

- What are you spending the most time on?
- Which of those activities directly impact your team's success or your customer's value?
- What can you eliminate, delegate, or redesign?

Smart Is the New Hard – Leading with Focus and Friction

Every leader eventually reaches a crossroads where they must choose between two paths:

- The path of pleasing everyone, avoiding conflict, and staying busy.
- The path of clarity, impact, and friction, where you challenge the flow, ask the hard questions, and protect your team's energy for what matters.

The second path isn't easy. But it's the one that builds sustainable success.

If the first part of leadership is learning to manage yourself, then the next is guiding others, not just by assigning tasks, but by shaping how they think, decide, and work.

This section is about stepping into that role.

The Trap of Task Leadership

Most managers operate in what I call Task Mode:

- Assign tasks
- Track deadlines
- Clear bottlenecks
- Push for more output

While Task Mode is necessary at times, it can quickly become toxic. Why? Because when everything is a task, nothing is a mission.

Teams become busy but not aligned. Exhausted but not empowered. They start confusing volume with value. And leaders unknowingly reward the wrong behaviors: staying late, taking on more, never saying no.

That's when you get burnout, not from a lack of ability, but from a lack of direction.

True leadership begins when you start operating in Friction Mode.

What is Friction Mode?

Friction Mode is when you choose to:

- Pause momentum to ask: "Is this the right thing?"
- Say no to low-impact work even when it's popular
- Realign work around goals, not just capacity
- Protect people from overwork by enforcing boundaries
- Redesign meetings and roles based on outcomes, not tradition

Friction Mode feels uncomfortable, especially at first.

It may create temporary resistance. People may feel you're slowing them down. But long-term, it builds clarity, focus, and trust.

Because teams ultimately want a leader who's not just watching them work, but ensuring that their work matters.

The Power of a Difficult No

A few years ago, I had a high-performing team that was deep into developing a new internal platform. They were passionate, driven, and logging long hours to hit deadlines.

Midway through development, I reviewed the evolving roadmap and asked, "How much does this reduce time-to-decision for our internal users?"

The answer wasn't clear. In fact, some features were adding complexity without reducing effort.

I suggested we drop a module that had already seen three weeks of design effort. The team pushed back, emotionally, not because they disagreed on logic, but because they felt attached to the work.

I understood.

But I had to make the call. We dropped it, redirected focus toward automations that directly reduced repetitive manual steps for users, and reallocated bandwidth to building analytics that helped managers make faster, smarter decisions.

Three months later, adoption rates were nearly 2X our earlier projections. Satisfaction scores shot up. The module we dropped was never missed.

The lesson?

Saying no to effort isn't disrespectful. It's leadership.

Redefining Leadership: From "Always On" to "Always Aligned"

The era of glorifying 18-hour days is fading. Smart organizations don't celebrate burnout; they design against it.

Here's how modern leaders think:

- They optimize for results, not optics
- They encourage teams to question priorities
- They protect time and energy like currency
- They reward clarity and courage, not just compliance

And they recognize that focus is the new hustle.

That means setting fewer, clearer priorities. It means letting go of the idea that being busy equals being valuable. It means creating space for recovery, reflection, and strategy.

Because nobody can sprint forever. And sprinting in the wrong direction is worse than walking in the right one.

Smart Work Requires Smart Conversations

If you want to move your team from hard work to smart work, you need to create an environment where strategic friction is safe.

Here's how:

1. Normalize Pausing

Encourage your team to stop and ask:

- "Why are we doing this?"
- "What happens if we don't?"
- "Does this still align with the goal?"

These pauses prevent waste. They build accountability. And they empower people to think, not just do.

2. Shift Language from Effort to Impact

Instead of asking, "How busy are you?" ask:

- "What outcome are you driving this week?"
- "Which task will move us closer to the goal?"

Language shapes mindset. If you focus on output, they'll focus on impact.

3. Protect Boundaries

Model rest, breaks, and saying no.

- Avoid late-night messages unless urgent.
- Question unnecessary meetings.
- Be vocal about prioritizing energy management.

When you protect your own energy, you give your team permission to do the same.

Toolbox: The Personal Brand Audit

You may be wondering, what does smart work have to do with personal branding?

Everything.

How people perceive your contribution, your leadership style, your value, and your influence is directly shaped by how you work.

Here's a quick audit. Ask yourself:

Question	Yes / No
Do others seek you out for strategic input, not just execution?	

Are you regularly tapped to solve business-critical problems?	
Is your name associated with clarity, not just hard work?	
Do people leave your meetings with more focus, not more confusion?	
Are you seen as a multiplier of energy and insight?	
Do you regularly review how your work aligns with business goals?	

The more "Yes" answers, the stronger your smart leadership brand.

If most are "No," don't panic; this is simply a prompt for evolution.

Smart work shapes how others talk about you when you're not in the room. That's your brand. That's your leverage.

Smart Work Culture: It Starts at the Top

Culture is what leaders consistently allow, reward, and demonstrate.

If you want your team to prioritize impact over activity:

- Reward people who say no to unaligned work
- Publicly appreciate strategic pivots, even if they delay delivery
- Share stories of measured outcomes, not just hustle

Create a safe space for friction. Where people can speak up about misaligned work, raise concerns about workload, or challenge assumed priorities.

Smart work culture is built when leaders stop praising the person who worked 80 hours and start recognizing the one who simplified a 10-hour process into two.

Letting Go of Guilt

One of the biggest hidden blockers to smart leadership?

Guilt.

We've been raised in school, in jobs, in families, to believe that hard work is a moral virtue. That rest is weakness. That saying no means selfishness.

Let me be clear:

- Smart work is not lazy.
- Prioritizing rest is not weak.
- Protecting your team's focus is not selfish.

It's leadership maturity.

And it's how you build a life, and a legacy, that doesn't collapse under the weight of its own effort.

Think about your current leadership pattern:

- Where are you rewarding effort over outcome?
- When was the last time you said no, and it made the work better?
- Are you protecting your team's energy, or just their tasks?
- Do people feel safe to challenge low-impact work?

Choose one small friction point this week. Lean into it. Ask the hard question. Pause a sprint. Challenge a meeting.

Start showing your team that smart is the new hard.

Chapter 3: The Dip is Inevitable

The day will come in any high-performing organization, be it business, sport, or school, when the buzz is out. It's unavoidable. Companies that operate under the constant strain, where objectives and demands are set aggressively and deadlines are unforgiving, will, sooner or later, end up with days or even weeks on end, when they lose motivation, drop morale, and start to decline in their production. The point is not whether this will or will not take place. It is when, and more to the point, what can you do about it?

When the Energy Slumps: Seeing the Moment

You may catch it first in the body language. People show up late. They remain silent in meetings. Emails are brief, chilly. Slack messages are utilitarian. Work gets completed, but the spark, the human energy that drives creativity and collaboration, is absent.

It's simple to overlook these warnings. In fact, the most likely reaction is to plow ahead, praying that the mood improves on its own. But faking it till it makes sense can be risky. A team that feels unheard and unseen can slide deeper into disengagement. Productivity may persist in the short run, but the ground starts to shift.

The Price of Pretend So, Everything is All Right

There is often an implicit condition of stoicism in high-performance cultures. Be tough. Don't whine. Work harder. There is nothing wrong with resilience, but feelings should not be suppressed. By denying the state of affairs that not everything is alright when indeed it is not the case, the leaders convey the unspoken code of a different message: there is no place here to be weak.

The price? No one speaks up. Problems languish. Good people exhaust themselves or leave. Leaders' credibility is undermined. And most sadly, chances for actual human connection, opportunities that could elevate the team, are lost.

The Benefits of Group Huddles: Why Athletes Do Group Huddles and Why Your Team Should Do It

Before a big play, sports teams huddle not because they are puzzled about what to do, but they do it because they need to bond. The huddle is an experience of communal energy, of and through eye contact, of we together are in this thing.

Such huddles in offices do not need to be complex. This can also be a 10-minute check-in, walk-and-talk, or a lunch break that does not involve sitting at desks. It's an opportunity to interrupt the pattern and recharge emotionally.

When energy is low, it's more often not about the work itself but about how individuals *feel* doing the work. Huddles are a reminder to individuals that they are not alone.

The Power of Vulnerability in High-Performance Environments

One of the most powerful things a leader can do in times of low energy is admit that they, too, feel it. Vulnerability isn't weakness; it's relatability. Saying something like, "I've noticed we're all a bit off lately. Let's talk about it," creates space for honesty.

When leaders demonstrate that they're human, they permit others to do the same. That vulnerability can be a breakthrough, not only in team spirit, but in results. Once feelings are recognized, they can be controlled.

Story: From Frustration to Fuel, A Recovery Arc

Take me back to a story I experienced on a project in Africa. We had a current customer engagement, and I was to visit the team for a quarterly update. The objective was straightforward: meet the team, lunch, and prep for the client meeting.

When I met the four team members, I was struck immediately by their faces. They were drained, not tired of late hours, but low in spirits. The kind of low you don't get from reading a status report.

I could tell they were eager to discuss, but didn't feel comfortable enough to open up. So, I changed things slightly. I moved the meeting from a hotel conference space to their guest home, where they'd been residing for six weeks. Rather than discussing business, we agreed they'd prepare lunch for us. They had learned how to cook simple meals, and I spoke of my initial attempts at cooking.

The atmosphere shifted. Giggles broke out. People talked. I inquired about how they were managing being distant from home and whether they liked the culture. At last, I inquired, "What's giving you trouble about the project?"

That's when it emerged: client site internal politics, misinformation, blame-shifting. They were being scapegoated for issues outside their control. What they were most afraid of was the meeting with the client's executive sponsor, someone they felt had been presented with incorrect information.

I did not give them a plan. I listened. Then we attended the meeting.

The air was charged. The client's team had prepared a presentation to lay out their view of the project status. I requested just a few minutes before they could proceed.

I began by thanking their team for receiving us, offering sincere appreciation, and emphasizing how much we'd gained from the engagement. I complimented the commitment of our team, away from home, working under unknown conditions.

Within 10 minutes, the atmosphere in the room changed. Our executive sponsor joined in, appreciating our team's dedication and efforts. The official presentation never materialized. We had an open, human discussion instead.

The client started working with our team, providing advice on how to work on internal dynamics. It was no longer about faulting; it was about assisting. Even the junior client staff member who was scheduled to present was instructed, "Let's forego that. This is more critical."

We walked out of the meeting, and my team had the look of a championship winner. They were charged, they were proud, and most importantly, they felt they had my support, and now, the client's.

The turnaround did not occur due to a grand strategy. It occurred because we slowed down, communicated, and made room for candor.

Toolbox

1. The Grit Grid

An easy-to-use framework to plot emotional highs and lows against team results. Assists you in recognizing patterns:

When our morale was high, what were we doing?

When our performance went down, what emotional cues did we miss?

What internal and external drivers correspond with team energy?

Use it in retrospectives to establish emotional awareness in performance monitoring.

2. "Crisis Conversations" Blueprint

When things are breaking down, this is a 3-step conversation template:

1. Acknowledge reality: "I know things are stressful at the moment."

2. Ask for honesty: "What's actually going on that we're not speaking out loud?"

3. Co-create a response: "What do we together need to shift?"

Don't rush problem-solving too soon. People must feel heard before they can take action.

3. How to Spot Low Energy in a Team Member

Body language: slouching shoulders, avoiding eye contact

Language: brief answers, defensiveness

Participation: backing away from conversation, low engagement

What re-energizes them:

- Changing context (get out of the meeting room)
- Humor and brief storytelling
- Reaffirming purpose: "Here's why this work matters."
- Personal attention: Ask how they're doing outside of work

Last Thoughts

Energy slumps are not a weakness; they're humanity. The best leaders aren't the ones who steer clear of them, but the ones who catch on early and respond with compassion, imagination, and connection.

At times, answers aren't hidden in the project plan or dashboard. At times, they're discovered in a guest house kitchen, over a humble home-cooked meal.

When unsure, don't ask what's wrong. Ask, "How are *you* doing?" Then listen, not to reply, but to comprehend.

That's how teams repair. That's how energy comes back. That's how champions are created.

Reading the Room – Lessons in Influence and Emotional Calibration

We've all walked into a room believing we know what's going on, only to be blindsided by a completely different vibe. The art of influence isn't just about what you say; it's about when you say it, how you say it, and most importantly, how you read the room before you say anything at all.

Let me share one such humbling experience, a story that taught me more about influence than a dozen leadership books ever could.

The Celebration That Wasn't

It was just after a company-wide payroll increment cycle had been concluded. On paper, everything looked great. The company had grown, our numbers were up, and we had just rolled out salary increases across levels. For me, this was a moment of optimism, a milestone that I believed would lift morale and energize teams.

So, I walked into the room with the energy of someone who had good news. You know the kind, light smile, confident body language, a sense of purpose. I was eager to meet the managers and hear how the changes had landed with their teams. I was expecting cheerful responses, a few claps, nods of agreement, maybe even a "Great job!" or two. Instead, what I walked into was a wall of silence.

Not complete silence, just that polite, neutral kind. You can sense it when people are being courteous but aren't emotionally with you. I pushed through with my message: "We've made good progress, the organization is growing, and this round of increments is a symbol of that. We're counting on our rejuvenated teams to take us to the next level!"

Still, barely any response. A couple of them nodded; one or two brought up some procedural concerns, employees being on leave or deployed at client locations who hadn't received the update yet. That was it.

That moment, when enthusiasm is met with a vacuum, is emotionally jarring. But it's also a pivotal test of leadership.

The Mirror Breaks

I realized quickly that I had misread the room. The managers weren't unhappy to see me. They weren't being rude. But my version of events, the 'celebration' I had walked in with, wasn't their lived experience. And to be fair, they hadn't had a chance to even process their own reactions yet.

Eventually, I paused and asked the most important question of that day: "What could we have done better?"

I'll never forget what followed. It was as if I had opened the lid of a pressure cooker. The concerns started flowing, not with anger but with honesty. The responses fell broadly into three categories:

1. Lack of involvement:
   Several managers felt the bell curve methodology used in the evaluation process had limited their discretion. They weren't truly part of the performance and reward calibration, so they didn't own the outcomes. Some even felt awkward facing their teams because they couldn't explain the "why" behind the hikes.

2. Not market-aligned:
   A few candidly mentioned that the overall increment percentage didn't reflect the market dynamics, especially in a year when inflation and talent movement were at an all-time high. "It's hard to call it a win when other companies are offering significantly more," one manager remarked.

3. Attrition risk:
   Almost everyone expressed worry that, despite the intention behind the hike, we hadn't done enough to retain key performers. A manager said, "We might see a few good people walk out over the next quarter. What's our plan to stop that?"

At that point, I knew this wasn't a session about celebration; it was a session about listening, regrouping, and reworking the narrative.

The Pivot

What surprised me most wasn't the feedback itself, but the emotional intelligence of the managers. They weren't complaining; they were offering insights, looking for a way to be part of the solution. The mistake I had made was coming into the meeting with my emotional dial turned too high, too soon. And I hadn't done the basic leadership work: read the room.

To recover, I shifted gears. I set aside my prepared notes and engaged in an open conversation. We spent the rest of the meeting dissecting their feedback, talking through edge cases, figuring out how we could do better next cycle, and how we could communicate more transparently with employees.

When we wrapped up, the energy in the room was completely different. It wasn't high-fives and applause, but it was grounded, sincere, and purposeful. We had co-created a sense of direction, and that was more powerful than any celebratory monologue I had prepared.

Influence Is Not Volume, It's Timing

That day taught me something critical: influence isn't always about being right, it's about being in rhythm.

Just like a musician doesn't start playing the drums without tuning into the band, a leader shouldn't start pushing messages before tuning into the emotional beat of the room.

From then on, I began every important team conversation with a short pause. Not a literal one always, but an internal scan. Observe who's making eye contact. Who looks relaxed, who looks tense. How are people greeting each other? What are they not saying?

I still bring the same smile and energy, but I've trained myself to withhold excitement until I can sense it will be received. I ask a few warm-up questions. I invite the room in before I take them anywhere.

Sometimes, I still get it wrong. But much less frequently.

Empowerment Through Empathy

Another shift that came out of that meeting was my approach to communication going forward. I began introducing my ideas with two things: acknowledgement of challenges and shared ownership of the solution. For example, instead of "This is great, let's keep going!" I would say: "I know the last few weeks have been a mix; some teams are thrilled, others are processing it differently. I want to hear from you, and also share what we've learned and what we can improve. This is a journey we're on together."

And the difference in response was dramatic.

When people feel seen and heard, they don't just engage, they commit. You give them the microphone, and they bring the music.

Influence Isn't a Speech. It's a Conversation.

In hindsight, my mistake in that meeting was simple: I came in with a message, not a conversation. Influence isn't a monologue; it's a shared experience. And every person in the room brings with them a history, a context, and an emotional map. If you ignore that, your words become noise. But if you honor it, your words carry meaning.

Self-Reflection

There's no universal formula for influence. But there is a universal truth:
You cannot lead people you don't listen to.

I learned that the hard way, but I'm grateful I did. Because of that meeting, which started off as a failure in emotional intelligence, ended up being one of the most pivotal conversations in my leadership journey.

It made me more human. And that, perhaps, is the greatest influence of all.

Charisma, Confidence, and the Human Aspect of Leadership in a Digital Age

As we construct smart, scalable, AI-first campuses and institutions capable of anticipating an ever-changing educational environment, we tend to think about architecture, compliance, data, and infrastructure quite a bit. But there's another type of infrastructure, one constructed of human beings, personality, and presence.

And within this human infrastructure, something intangible but potent resides: charisma.

Charisma is not necessarily on the list of campus KPIs, but in staff rooms, classrooms, boardrooms, and job interviews, charisma can be the key to being listened to and heard, or ignored. It's the hidden cue that sets people straight when you talk, that adds gravity to your words, and turns ideas into movements.

But here's the question we're examining today: Is charisma teachable?

No One Is Born Charismatic

We tend to call some individuals "naturally charismatic", the ones who just step into a room and immediately capture hearts. But the truth is, charisma is more often a learned ability than a birthright. It's an acquired skill. An honed talent.

Some do have an advantage. Consider a child who is raised in a family of politicians, public speakers, or business leaders; these children are surrounded by communication, confidence, and presence as normal, everyday routines. It's not magic, it's muscle memory created from years of immersion.

But for the rest of us, those who weren't born and raised at the dinner tables of senators or CEOs, charisma is still accessible. We just have to construct it, one habit at a time.

So, What Is Charisma, Really?

Charisma is not charm or extroversion. It's not about talking over everyone in the room or being the loudest person in the room. It's a subtle blend of three essential ingredients:

Confidence

Enthusiasm

Optimism

Let's deconstruct these, not only as ideas, but as trainable, measurable, and actionable competencies.

1. Confidence: Faith in Self, Not Expertise

Confidence is not about knowing everything. Confidence is believing that you have something worth contributing, even if you're still learning.

We too frequently believe that we must be experts in the subject matter before we speak. Confidence is not perfection. Its presence.

You don't have to know it all. You just have to own what you know.

Trainable Confidence Habits:

Practice standing up straight, back straight, shoulders back, chest open.

Make eye contact, not a stare-down, but with warmth and intent.

Don't use filler words. Practice pausing rather than rushing.

Listen actively and validate others' contributions before responding.

Share ideas with curiosity, not fear.

One underappreciated confidence-builder? Innovate in conversation. Be the one who brings a new perspective or the one who asks a question that interrupts the conversation. That subtle move conveys leadership, even at a dinner party.

And don't forget: confidence isn't about being loud. It's about being clear.

2. Enthusiasm: Positive Energy in Action

Enthusiasm is the interpersonal manifestation of internal joy. It's the spark you bring into a room. It's contagious, and people are drawn to it.

When you enter a room and greet individuals with sincere warmth, a firm handshake, and a smile that reaches your eyes, people pay attention. You don't need to tell jokes every two minutes, but humor and levity have a great deal of carry in making you memorable and attractive.

Trainable Enthusiasm Habits:

Rehearse saying people's names in dialogue.

Come in early, not on time, as this conveys intention and enthusiasm.

Dress thoughtfully. Not excess, just simplicity and pride.

Be the first to say "Hi." Break the ice.

Employ tone, gestures, and voice modulation to demonstrate your care.

In a corporate world where so many wear beige, enthusiasm stands out in color.

3. Optimism: The Discipline of Positivity

Charisma isn't solely about arriving with confidence and energy; it's where you're willing to place your focus.

Optimism is not naivety. It's deciding to see potential even in challenges. It's a skill of reeling in the story so others feel hopeful when they're around you.

Consider it: Would you rather walk behind someone who utters, "This is a disaster," or someone who utters, "Here's where the opportunity is"?

Trainable Optimism Habits:

In each meeting, attempt to begin with a positive observation.

When providing feedback, take a "Yes, and" attitude rather than "But."

Don't deny the negatives, just put the positives first.

Celebrate small wins. Speak up about appreciation.

Optimism creates trust. When others feel that you can contain challenges without falling apart, they begin to trust you as a leader. That's charisma at work.

My Story: From Self-Doubt to Presence

I was 29, and suddenly I found myself in executive management meetings with an average age of 45. I had great ideas, particularly regarding customer knowledge. One-to-one, I could converse beautifully. But the minute we got into those stodgy boardrooms, I'd shut down.

I doubted myself. I'd rehearse what I was going to say 10 times before opening my mouth, for fear of sounding junior or off-point. It wasn't that I wasn't knowledgeable. I wasn't confident.

Little by little, I began to watch the others talk. How they worded things. But I made it clear to myself that I didn't want to copy anyone else. I wanted to be me, just improved.

My superpower was understanding the customer. So I doubled down on that. I figured out how to frame even hard messages, like risk of churn or product deficiencies, as opportunities. I rehearsed how to deliver it with body language that was friendly but firm.

And something changed. Eventually, after a while, when I talked, the room would fall silent. Folks began waiting to hear my perspective. Eventually, I got to the point where they'd say, "What do you think we should do next?"

That's when I knew, this is charisma in a meeting room.

Not acting. Not narcissism. Just faith, predicated on clear thinking, positive thinking, and genuine excitement.

Why This Matters on an AI-First Campus

You may ask, what does charisma have to do with AI and future-ready campuses?

Everything.

Because AI can make systems run better. It can digitize workflow, tailor learning, cut down data, and even match students to a career. But it can't motivate.

That's what people do.

Leaders, professors, student mentors, and even classmates all depend on some charisma to connect, persuade, and lead.

As campuses go digital, the human factor is more valuable than ever. We don't require merely confident thinkers. We require confident communicators.

So let's not merely spend on software and systems when we consider how to create a digital-first campus. Let's spend on skills such as:

Presentation and storytelling training

Role-playing tough conversations

Executive presence coaching

Peer feedback cycles for soft skill building

These aren't "nice to have." They're must-haves.

Your Charisma Blueprint

To sum it all up, charisma is not some intangible trait possessed by a select few. It's a blend of:

Confidence – Understanding and embracing your worth

Enthusiasm – Arriving with energy and purpose

Optimism – Positing the future with hope and potential

If you can cultivate these, you can enter any room, communicate in any meeting, confront any customer, and leave individuals remembering not only what you said, but how you made them feel.

In the era of AI and automation, charisma may be your most human and most valuable superpower.

Development Toolkit: Confidence, Enthusiasm, Optimism in Action

1. The Confidence Builder Kit

Goal: Train your mind and body to project calm self-belief, even in unfamiliar territory.

Tools & Practices:

- Daily Power Pose (2 mins): Stand tall, shoulders back, hands on hips. Do this before key meetings. It signals strength to your brain.
- "I Know My Value" Log: Write down one strength or success daily. Reflect on what makes you unique in your role.

- The 5-Second Rule: Count backward 5–4–3–2–1 before speaking up. It helps bypass self-doubt and take action in meetings.
- Confidence through Curiosity: You don't have to know everything. Ask smart, open-ended questions, and people will remember your curiosity as insight.

Watch Out: Confidence isn't volume. It's clarity. Speak calmly, make eye contact, pause often. That's more powerful than rushing.

<u>2. The Enthusiasm Amplifier Kit</u>

Goal: Energize the room and make others feel seen, heard, and valued.

Tools & Practices:

- The 3-Point Connect: When entering a room, make it a habit to:
    1. Smile and greet at least 3 people.
    2. Ask one personal/non-work question.
    3. Find and name something you admire (a project, outfit, idea)
- Energy Audit: Notice what drains or excites you. Align 80% of your day with high-energy tasks. You can't fake enthusiasm forever if you're running on empty.

- Enthusiasm Sandwich: Start and end every presentation or update on a high note (positive news, excitement about the future), sandwiching tough messages in the middle.
- Be the Icebreaker: Always carry 2–3 light, thoughtful conversation starters. (Example: "What's the most exciting thing you're working on right now?")

3. The Optimism Discipline Kit

Goal: Become the one who sees opportunity even in adversity, and helps others see it too.

Tools & Practices:

- The Reframe Practice: When facing a challenge, write down the negative first. Then force yourself to find three possible upsides. (Example: A tough client issue might become a case study or a chance to improve the product.)
- Optimism Language Swap:
    - Instead of "This is a mess," try "This is complex, but solvable."
    - Instead of "We failed," try "We learned something critical."
    - Instead of "That won't work," try "What would make that work?"

- Gratitude Huddle (weekly): In team meetings, take 2 mins to share one win or moment of gratitude. It rewires brains to see progress.
- Sunlight First: Start your day with 5 minutes in sunlight or fresh air. It naturally boosts dopamine and optimism.

<u>4. Charisma in Meetings Kit</u>

Goal: Become the person everyone listens to and wants to hear from again.

Tools & Practices:

- 30-Second Rule: When you speak, try to make your point clearly in under 30 seconds before elaborating. This helps command attention.
- The Positive Setup: Even when delivering tough news, start with: "Here's what's working..." or "Here's the opportunity I see..."
- Suggest the Next Step: End every comment with a solution or question that drives the discussion forward. "What if we tried this?" or "Shall I explore that option further?"
- Watch for the Glance: People glance at those they trust. Observe who others look to when unsure, and become that person over time through presence and consistency.

5. The Charisma Journal (Weekly Reflection Tool)

Every Friday, answer these 5 questions:

1. When did I feel most confident this week?
2. What gave me energy? What drained it?
3. How did I turn a negative into a positive?
4. Who did I connect with deeply, and how?
5. What one thing will I do better next week?

Final Thought

Charisma isn't about being the loudest voice in the room. It's about being the clearest, calmest, and most constructive. It's how you make people feel seen, supported, and inspired. And every one of these skills can be practiced.

Start small. Be consistent. Watch your presence transform.

Chapter 4: Keep Showing Up

There's a quiet form of leadership nobody discusses nearly enough. It doesn't have glitzy titles, public proclamations, or epic turnarounds. It's the type that remains when others depart. That stays present when nobody has a clue what to say. That keeps showing up, repeatedly, even when the spotlights faded out. Especially then.

Most of the time, we lose sight of leadership and instead equate it to jumping in headstrong, motivating others, or being the biggest talker in the room. But the moments that some leadership is etched in by the most are the moments when you are standing still-alone, and yet you decide to remain.

Not The Hero

You know what it feels like when you try to lead a team through unknown, confusion, or change. You are not a scriptwriter. You are the sticking agent. You are the person who collects the pieces together when things are disintegrating around us.

Leading from the middle is never sexy. There are no headlines announcing how you facilitated two departments finally communicating with one another. There will never be a case study praising the 87th check-in you ever did with your team to boost morale in a downturn. This is where trust is forged. This is where true culture resides, not in posters or values decks, but in the daily drudge of being there.

And this type of showing up? It's contagious.

The Day I Had to Smile Through a Storm

Several years ago, we had recently celebrated a milestone: our company had been acquired by a big US company. There was euphoria in the air. I was delighted, revved up with the thought that what we did had resulted in something worthwhile. I spoke to my team in India, broke the news to them with all the enthusiasm I could, and then caught a flight to America to meet the new leadership.

The initial day was all I dreamed it would be, meetings full of vision, collaboration, and possibility. I met the new CEO. I shook hands with board members. I felt like we were at the threshold of something great. That night, over dinner, the CEO pulled me aside for what I imagined would be a strategy discussion.

Instead, he dropped a bomb.

We don't want the India business," he declared bluntly. "It doesn't align with our model."

I blinked, attempting to process the words. Was this a miscommunication?

He went on, matter-of-factly, "If you can sell it, okay. Otherwise, you'll have to start phasing it out in 4 to 5 months."

Just like that.

I flew back the following day, sitting in that airplane seat, trying to convince myself how to muster a brave face for my team. They were eager, optimistic, looking for tales of expansion and world ambitions. I was coming back with none of those things. I was coming back with silence and devastation.

You Don't Get to Quit

What that taught me was something I'll never forget: leadership is staying, even when your heart aches to flee.

I had no idea what was next. But I did know this: I owed it to my team to be present for them. Not with deceit. Not with broken promises. But with calm. With intention. With presence.

I delayed the team meeting. I did not want to present to them half-truths. Instead, I spoke with my inner circle, went over our limited choices, and began searching for possible purchasers, quietly but with fierce determination.

For the next few months, it was like living a double life, keeping morale high on one hand and scouting every possible lead on the other. There were days when I'd leave a brainstorming session about our next internal project and step into a phone call with a potential acquirer.

But here's the thing: humans sense energy. They can't always put it into words, but they can tell when a leader's around. And they can tell when you've bailed, even though your body is still in the room.

So, I remained. Not physically. Mentally. Emotionally. I showed up to team standups. I showed up to one-on-ones. I showed up to celebratory moments and client pitches, even when I had no idea if we'd be around in six months.

We did eventually locate a buyer. The company endured. A lot of jobs were preserved. But even if that hadn't occurred, I know this: the group understood that I didn't leave them behind. And that's more important than any merger.

Recovery Habits: Team Energy Rituals

Leadership in chaos isn't pretending that everything is okay. It's about instilling tiny rituals that remind your team of their power, even during adversity.

One of the things we began during that tough time was a weekly "micro-win" huddle. Friday, 15 minutes. One thing each person did well. It was as simple as making a successful call, having a new idea, or getting through a difficult week.

We also initiated a 3-minute "energy check" in our Monday meetings. Everyone rated their energy level out of 10. It became a surprisingly powerful way to spot who was running low, who needed support, and who could lend energy to the rest.

These rituals don't cost a thing. But they become anchors in stormy waters.

What Do They Say When You're Not in the Room?

Here's a penetrating question for any leader: What do your team members say about you when you're not in the room?

Not the LinkedIn version. Not the buzzwords in a 360-review. The real deal.

Do they say you freak out under pressure, or that you bring poise?

Do they say you listen, or that you disappear when it gets tough?

Do they feel like they matter to you?

The reality of your leadership isn't in your CV. It's in what people say about you when you're not around.

It's Okay Not to Be Strong All the Time

Honestly, being a leader is draining. It's isolating. And there will be times when you don't wish to be the strong one.

There were nights throughout that acquisition period when I was sitting in my car after work just staring at the steering wheel, not knowing if I would be able to walk back in tomorrow and wear the same tough face.

But leadership is not about being tough all the time. It's about being present even when you don't feel strong. It's about believing in the culture you have in place to carry each other through. You don't have to do it by yourself. But you do need to be there.

Like a Parent, Only You Can't Tuck the Team into Bed

Leadership is very much like parenthood. You experience anticipation, pride, worry, frustration, happiness, all in one day. And then comes that moment, just a single quiet hug, one word of appreciation, one smile from someone who says, "I hung in there because of you."

That's the moment you know: this is worth it. And I wouldn't have it any other way.

The Courage to Stay

In a culture that adores speed, disruption, and daring action, we lose sight of the quiet strength of sticking around. Of loyalty. Being with your people when the story gets complicated and the solutions aren't apparent.

But if you want to create enduring trust, genuine, real trust, you have to be present.

Even when you don't know everything.

Even when your heart is shattered.

Even when you're the sole survivor.

Because when you arrive like that, you're giving your team license to do the same.

And that's when the magic occurs.

Why real leadership means staying when others leave

The story picks up with me walking back into the India office after that turbulent trip to the U.S. My mind was in overdrive. I was still processing the brutal reality that the India business, once celebrated, once integral, was now considered expendable. But leadership isn't about passing on the panic. It's about presence. It's about the choice to stay calm, clear, and courageous, even when the ground beneath you is shaking.

The Art of Showing Up When It Hurts

Here I was, standing in front of the team. These were people who had built the business with their bare hands and beating hearts. Many of them had spent years with us, poured their weekends into product releases, missed family events to meet deadlines, and taken pride in what they had created. And now they looked at me, eyes wide with anticipation, expecting good news.

And I had none to give.

Not yet, at least.

But I couldn't break that trust, not by omission, not by panic, not by transferring my own fear onto them. Leadership, especially in times like this, is about how you hold the space. So I leaned into honesty, but with hope. I started by painting the big picture: the acquisition, the opportunities, the global platform we now had access to.

Then I turned the spotlight on them. I reminded them of what got us to this point. "This company was valued the way it was because of you," I said. "Because of the intelligence, integrity, and commitment that this team in India brought to the table every single day."

You could see the shift in the room. Shoulders straightening. Eyes glinting with pride.

When You Don't Have All the Answers

Of course, I didn't tell them everything that night. Not because I was hiding the truth, but because we weren't ready yet. I had four to five months to figure out how to save this business. What they needed from me right now wasn't a problem; they needed purpose.

So, I offered a path forward. I told them I would be working closely with our former CEO, who was still an advisor. I positioned this transition period as an incubation phase for something bigger. I asked for their trust. "What we need right now is for everyone to keep doing what you've always done: deliver exceptional service. Give our customers no reason to doubt us."

Glue, Not the Hero

In these moments, you realise what it means to lead from the middle. Not as the loudest voice in the room. Not as the visionary with all the answers. But as the glue, the quiet force that holds things together when they feel like they're falling apart.

There's a misconception about leadership. People think it's about heroic speeches, bold strategies, charismatic turns. But real leadership is often quieter. It's about consistency. Showing up. Especially on the hard days. Especially when your voice shakes. Especially when you're not sure if you'll win.

That's what I tried to do: be the person they could look at and feel anchored. That week, I had one-on-one chats with key team members. I checked in on people. I spent time on the floor, casually joining team lunches, cracking jokes in meetings, and being there. My presence became my power.

Creating Rituals of Resilience

I knew we had a storm to weather, so we needed rituals, anchors of energy that would help the team stay hopeful. We introduced small weekly wins meetings every Friday. We didn't talk strategy. We just celebrated progress. A client appreciation email. A bug that got fixed. A junior team member who stepped up. These micro-wins gave people something to look forward to.

We also did "energy check-ins" at the beginning of key meetings. One word: how are you feeling today? Not as a performance metric, but as a pulse check. It created psychological safety. It let people know that whatever they were carrying, they didn't have to carry it alone.

Those rituals mattered. They reminded people that we're human beings first, employees second.

The Power of Transparent Optimism

Over the next few weeks, we worked like our future depended on it, because it did. Behind the scenes, I was talking to potential investors, evaluating buyers, and lobbying for the India team's capabilities. But on the ground, I was building something else, trust. Not the fluffy kind, but the kind that's earned when you tell people the truth, involve them in the mission, and give them reasons to believe.

I didn't promise guarantees. I promised effort. I didn't sugarcoat uncertainty. I painted possibilities. I didn't lead with power. I led with presence.

The Turnaround

Eventually, we did find a buyer for the India business. But it wasn't a rescue story; it was a rebirth story. The new company valued what we had built. They saw potential, not problems. Over the next few years, we didn't just survive, we grew. 15 times over.

But ask me what I remember most about that phase, and it's not the business metrics.

It's the moment someone said, "You never left."
It's the quiet conversations in the hallway.
It's the Friday wins meetings where someone's success got a standing ovation.
It's the junior analyst who said, "I want to lead like you someday."

You Can't Please Everyone – And You Shouldn't Try

One of the most difficult truths in leadership is this: you will never please everyone. No matter how well-intentioned or strategic your decision, there will always be someone who disagrees, resists, or feels left out. That's the nature of leading; it involves direction, change, and sometimes discomfort.

The goal of leadership is not to be liked by all; it is to do what is right for the mission, the team, and the long-term vision. When leaders fall into the trap of seeking universal approval, they dilute decisions, delay action, and lose credibility. Leadership is not a popularity contest; it's a responsibility to act in the best interest of the whole, even if that means a few people will be unhappy in the short term.

Equally important is how decisions are made. In any leadership role, you're constantly surrounded by noise, opinions, assumptions, rumors, and hearsay. It's easy to get swayed by what people are saying in the corridors or on group chats. But strong leadership is anchored in facts, not gossip. You owe it to your team to gather accurate information, consider the context, and apply judgment without bias or emotional reaction.

Make your decisions based on what you know, not what you hear. And once a decision is made, own it. Communicate it clearly. Be open about the reasoning, even if it's not what everyone wanted to hear. Transparency earns more respect than appeasement.

In short:

- You're not here to be everyone's favorite.
- You're here to move things forward with clarity and courage.

- Make informed decisions. Stick by them. And never let hearsay cloud your leadership.

Reflection: What Do They Say When You're Not in the Room?

Leadership isn't about what you say in the room. It's what people say when you're not there.

Do they say you panic when things go wrong? Or do they say you stay steady?
Do they say you take credit? Or that you share it?
Do they say you disappear in crises? Or that you show up, sleeves rolled?

Your legacy as a leader is built not in the good times, but in the messy middle. The uncertain middle. The 'are-we-gonna-make-it?' middle.

And if you can keep showing up there? You've already won half the battle.

The Silent Strength of Trust

How do you establish trust in a team struggling under pressure or recovering from failure? It's something I have questioned time and again over the years, particularly in the most uncertain moments of leadership.

Let me start off by saying this: you don't measure trust, you feel it. There's no gauge that lights up green when trust is strong or red when it's shattered. Trust is just in the background, like air in a room; you don't know it's there until it's gone.

You could conduct surveys, measure engagement metrics, or request 360-degree feedback. And yes, those provide signals. But the trust of a team shows itself in pressure situations. When things are going wrong, do they look to you or away from you? That's your mirror.

Trust Rests on Two Pillars: Competence and Warmth

Through experience, I've come to believe that trust simplifies to two pillars: competence and warmth.

As a leader, they must be able to see that you're capable of navigating the ship. If there is a storm brewing, they must have confidence that you possess both the radar and the compass. Competence wins them their respect.

Competence is insufficient, though. You must also generate emotional safety, which is where warmth enters. It's the feeling that you have an interest in your people, not merely their productivity. That you notice the human person behind the job title.

Now here's the twist: not everyone in your team has equal access to your warmth or your workstyle. Some would only talk to you in review meetings; others might just catch a glimpse of you on a town hall stage. So how do you trust in such asymmetric relationships?

For me, the answer is consistency.

Why Consistency Is the Bedrock of Trust

Consistency is underappreciated. Amidst the turmoil of change, individuals seek to be able to depend on things. A leader who consistently shows up the same way, whether it's amidst crisis or celebration, is that anchor.

My teams have grown to count on me delivering the following:

I'm always customer-first. I will ask how a decision affects the client, whether we're in a sales meeting, a hiring call, or an internal offsite.

I'm fiercely protective of revenue and retention. Even when the mood is relaxed, I'll pull us back to the numbers. This may sound rigid, but it helps people stay focused and sharp.

I prepare thoroughly for every meeting. If we're walking into a customer pitch, I've probably read the deck three times and made notes. If it's an internal presentation, I've already anticipated which slide will make me pause.

When you arrive in this way, day after day, it sends a message: "I might not always share your opinion, but you'll never be surprised at how I react." That reliability, particularly in uncertain times, is a kind of psychological safety.

The Power of Critical Feedback (With a Safety Net)

Yet another way I've established trust is by the way I offer feedback.

Here's an example. Suppose a team member comes into my office with a pitch deck. Before I reach slide two, I'll interrupt and say, "What's the single thesis here? Is this actually what the client is really looking for?" It comes across as blunt, perhaps even threatening. But the people get to know me and realize that I am not here to destroy them. I am here to raise the bar.

I don't sugarcoat. I'll tell you straight out, even if it's criticism, but always with a path forward. It's never "This doesn't work"; it's "This can be made stronger if you look at it this way."

Actually, I think trust is built when people realize that you care enough to push them. That you have their growth, not just their productivity, on your mind.

Celebrating Small Wins, And the Value of Chocolate Bars

One thing I've consciously done over the years is to celebrate small wins. Not just the big milestones or quarterly results, but the little things, like a well-handled client call, a tough conversation that ended positively, or a new idea that sparked excitement.

Sometimes that celebration is a chocolate bar. Other times, just a smile, a pat on the back, or a note of appreciation in front of the team.

You'd be amazed at how much one gesture can do. A member of staff reminded me one day, "I still recall when you came over with a Dairy Milk following my first presentation. I was terrified, but that moment made me realize I was part of the team."

These moments aren't about the present. They're about what it signifies: I notice you. I appreciate you. I celebrate you.

Failure: The True Test of Trust

Of course, the true test of trust isn't when everything goes right, but when it goes wrong.

Teams facing pressure tend to doubt, not only themselves, but their leaders. They ask themselves, "Will I be blamed? Will I be protected? Will I be heard?"

From my experience, the last thing you can do as a leader in the midst of failure is to become quiet. Or worse, blame. That's when trust is lost at lightning speed.

But instead, I've found it helpful to:

Admit the failure openly, without defensiveness.

Bring others into the process of getting it fixed, so they feel a sense of ownership of the turnaround.

Provide a constructive way forward, even if it's just the first few steps.

Sometimes it's just confronting reality: sometimes, that comes in the form of hard conversations. And even on those days, I try to provide a script: "This didn't work, but here's how we can bounce back."

That's how people remember it. Not that they failed, but that they were permitted to fail and still progress.

Providing the Space to Bounce Back

We often talk about giving people "space" to grow. But do we give people space to fail and bounce back?

In my leadership journey, I've made a point to make it explicit: You will not get disciplined for a mistake unless you make it again without learning. That line makes all the difference.

It permits. People to experiment. To challenge the edge. And most importantly, to bring their entire self to the workplace, imperfections and all.

This approach also helps build horizontal trust, where team members trust each other, not just the leader. When they see that failure is not fatal, they start backing each other, covering for each other, and sharing more freely.

That, to me, is the true culture of trust.

What I've Learned Over 30 Years

Reflecting on nearly three decades of working alongside teams, I don't pretend to have it all figured out. But I do know this: trust is built day by day.

It's built into how you show up when things get tough. In how you praise others when no one is around. In how you correct the course without shaming. And in how you say, "I've got your back", and mean it.

I've had teams approach me with fear in their eyes, and I've said to them, "We'll get through this together." And we did.

I've had presentations fail, deals fall through, and people quit. But the ones who remained, they remained not because everything was fine, but because they believed in the intent.

They understood that in the midst of chaos, I'd be consistent.

They understood that in criticism, I'd be fair.

And above all, they knew that when they lost, they wouldn't lose alone.

Trust Is a Reflection of Ourselves, in the End

So, if you're attempting to establish trust within your team, especially in the aftermath of failure, begin by looking in the mirror.

Ask yourself:

- Am I consistent in the way I lead, no matter the circumstances?
- Do I provide feedback with honesty and empathy?
- Do I celebrate the little successes just as much as the major ones?
- Do I create room for folks to fail and get back up?
- Do I show up, not only as a leader, but as a human?

If the answer is yes, trust will follow. Quietly, over time, and with great power.

Because in the end, trust is not something you say, it's something you demonstrate. Again, and again.

Turning Setbacks into Strengths – The Rituals of Recovery

Every successful organization knows how to celebrate a win. The emails fly, the congratulatory emojis pour in, and there's that unmistakable buzz in the air. But what truly separates resilient, future-ready institutions from the rest is not how they cheer the victories, but how they process their losses.

In the journey to build AI-first educational institutions or future-ready enterprises, setbacks are not just likely; they are inevitable. From a missed partnership, a failed rollout, a dropped opportunity, or worse, the loss of a high-value customer, there will be moments that test the resolve of even the strongest teams. It is in these moments that leadership either becomes real or reveals its hollowness.

Let's talk about what it means to really lead through a setback, and not just any setback, but the kind that knocks the air out of a team. Picture this: You've spent a year working with your team on the largest sales opportunity your company has ever seen. It's not just a number on the board, it's a symbol. Of trust. Of hard work. Of ambition. And then, right when you thought it was within reach, the deal goes to someone else.

Now what?

The Anatomy of a Fall

The loss of a major customer or opportunity is not a solitary event. It reverberates. Across desks. Across calendars. Across moods. Everyone, especially those closely involved, feels it. And the questions begin. "What went wrong?" "Could we have done better?" "Did we miss something?" These questions are not just analytical, they're personal.

For the team that was at the center of the opportunity, the emotional weight is immense. From being treated like rockstars internally, priority access, visibility at all levels, support from every function, they now have to wear the invisible tag of "the team that lost the deal." Worse, they must explain themselves over and over again to stakeholders who may mean well but don't fully understand the grind that went into the effort.

So, how do you help your team carry this weight, and more importantly, walk through it?

Step 1: Don't Just Talk to the Leader. Talk to the Whole Team.

My first instinct in a moment like this is to reach out not just to the team leader but to every person who played a role. This is not the time for filtered communication. Everyone who was emotionally and mentally invested in the opportunity deserves direct acknowledgment. I call a meeting, not to interrogate, but to reflect.

The tone of this conversation is everything. It's not about "what didn't work?" but "how are you doing?" It's not about "what's the damage?" but "what did we learn?" The message is simple: "You showed up. You gave your best. This didn't go our way, but it doesn't define your worth or your future."

Step 2: Acknowledge Their Work, Not Just the Result

One of the most harmful habits in corporate life is attaching appreciation only to success. But great teams are not made in winning moments; they're made in effort, collaboration, and relentless pursuit of a goal. In that meeting, I made it a point to highlight the amazing effort the team put in: how they prepared, collaborated across functions, brought in external experts, and showed up day after day with optimism and rigour.

I often share stories from the past, of other deals we lost, and how those very same teams rebounded stronger, went on to win even bigger opportunities. When people feel like their setback is part of a larger shared journey, they stop feeling isolated.

Step 3: Don't Sugarcoat, Make Room for Grief and Anger

Let's be honest. Sometimes, people just want to vent. About how close they were. About how unfair it felt. About the email they read at 2 a.m. that gave them false hope. And that's okay. A setback, especially a big one, has to be processed emotionally before it can be analyzed intellectually.

I give the team room to speak. I let the emotions breathe. There's no need to rush into solution-mode. Only when that emotional steam is released can you get into problem-solving mode without causing resentment or burnout.

Step 4: Debrief with Compassion and Clarity

After the dust has settled, usually a day or two later, we sit down again. This time, the tone shifts slightly. We talk about the experience, not the result. In the case of the lost Singapore deal, we looked at whether we were misled or if there was a blind spot we failed to notice. The answers weren't always comfortable, but the honesty was healing.

From there, we moved into what I call a "narrative reset." What's the story we want to tell the rest of the organization? Because trust me, people will ask. A setback this visible will travel. So, it's our responsibility to manage the message, not by spinning, but by reframing.

Step 5: Crafting a Communication Plan Together

One of the most empowering exercises post-setback is to involve the team in designing the communication. Who will inform which stakeholder? What tone will we adopt? What lessons will we highlight?

During the Singapore deal loss, I personally took the responsibility of informing the CEO, CFO, and key executives. Meanwhile, team members communicated with their respective counterparts. We didn't pretend everything was fine. Instead, we shared what we learned: how cross-team collaboration has improved, how we now have better systems for real-time information sharing, and how this experience has made us more prepared for the next big opportunity.

By the time we wrapped the meeting, nearly three hours long, you could visibly see the shift in body language. The shame and exhaustion gave way to a kind of clarity, even quiet confidence. The story they would carry out into the organization was no longer one of loss; it was one of resilience, growth, and a steely readiness for the next challenge.

Step 6: Recovery Plans Aren't Optional, They're Everything

Empathy is critical. But beyond that, your team looks to you for recovery. A plan. A next step. A goalpost to reach toward. As a leader, your job is not just to provide a shoulder to cry on; it's to build the ladder they can climb out of.

This is where you lay out a short-term and long-term plan. Maybe that means focusing on a new region, sharpening pricing strategies, or revisiting proposal methodologies. But it must be something real, tangible, and shared.

You don't just move on. You move forward, together.

Step 7: Institutionalize the Ritual of Setback Reviews

What we did with that team after the Singapore deal, we now do as a norm. Every significant loss, whether a customer, a talent, or a strategic opportunity, is followed by a ritual. We call them "Setback Reviews." Not to dwell, but to metabolize. Not to blame, but to grow.

In these reviews, we ask:

- What assumptions did we carry into this that didn't hold up?
- Which signals did we misread or ignore?
- What did we do better than ever before?
- What will we never do the same way again?

This ritual sends a powerful message across the organization: Here, we don't fear failure. We learn from it. Together.

Final Thoughts: Setbacks Are Not Signs of Weakness, They're Proof of Trying

Let me leave you with this: No great institution, product, or idea has emerged without its share of stumbles. In fact, the bolder your mission, the sharper the chances of failing at some point. But it is how you show up in these moments, and more importantly, how you help your team recover, that defines your leadership.

The next time your team loses something valuable, a deal, a client, a competition, remember: the goal is not just to soothe their wounds. It is to turn those wounds into wisdom. To hold up a mirror that reflects not just what was lost, but what was gained: tenacity, trust, and the unshakable belief that the next mountain is theirs to climb.

Because in future-ready campuses and organizations, failure is not the end of the road.

Toolkit: Building a Resilient Team Culture

This toolkit is designed to help leaders and teams process setbacks, retain morale, and build a stronger, more connected organization from every challenge faced.

1. Post-Setback Reflection Framework

Use this structure to help teams analyze, accept, and learn from difficult situations.

- What happened? Encourage the team to put facts on the table without judgment or blame.
- What did we control vs. not control? This helps reduce unnecessary guilt or over-responsibility.
- What went well despite the outcome? Salvage positives, such as team collaboration, speed, or improved relationships.
- What blind spots did we uncover? Identify areas where assumptions were made or feedback was missed.
- What can we do differently next time? Close the loop with actionable learnings that can be integrated into future plans.

2. Rituals to Normalize Setbacks

- "Lessons from the Field" Monthly Meetings: Rotate team members to present a project that didn't go as planned and share key lessons, no blame, just learning.
- "Failure Debrief Fridays": A casual, optional 30-minute end-of-week session where people can reflect on small or large setbacks.

- Leadership Storytelling Sessions: Leaders share stories from their own careers where things fell apart, and what came after.
- Win/Loss Wall: A visual board (physical or digital) that tracks major wins and losses along with a brief "What We Learned."

3. Communication Plan Builder for Setbacks

Use this to help teams navigate difficult internal or external messaging:

- Acknowledge the news: Be upfront and direct. Avoid sugarcoating.
- Appreciate the journey: Recognize the team's effort and growth, not just the outcome.
- Frame the impact: Share the broader implications honestly, both business and emotional.
- Share the plan forward: What's next? What are we doing with this learning?
- Assign responsibility for cascade: Who is informing which stakeholders? Map it clearly to avoid duplication or silence.

4. Leader's Checklist for Setback Conversations

Before you address the team, run through this:

1. Have I emotionally processed the situation myself?
2. Do I understand what mattered most to the team?
3. Am I showing empathy and clarity of direction?
4. Can I name at least 2–3 things we learned and improved?
5. Is the next step realistic and energizing?

5. Language to Use in the Moment

Words matter, especially in hard times. Here's some leader-friendly language:

- "I know this hurts, and that's okay." Acknowledges emotion without fixing it too quickly.
- "This doesn't erase all the good work we've done." Reinforces value beyond the result.
- "We now know what we couldn't have known earlier." Softens the blow of hindsight bias.
- "We're not the same team we were six months ago. Look how far we've come." Encourages forward-facing energy.

6. Team Rituals to Reignite Energy Post-Setback

- Recommit Session: A short meeting where each member shares one thing they're excited to work on next.
- Appreciation Circle: Everyone expresses one thing they admired in a teammate during the tough period.
- New Mission Kickoff: Close the loop on the past and open a fresh opportunity with symbolic weight (a new deck, a quote, a banner, etc.)

7. Resources for Ongoing Resilience

- Books:
  - The Obstacle Is the Way by Ryan Holiday
  - Option B by Sheryl Sandberg and Adam Grant
  - Radical Candor by Kim Scott
- Tools:
  - Retrospective.io or Miro boards for structured post-mortems
  - Slack channels like #failures-to-learn
  - Journaling templates for teams

- People:
    - Assign internal "resilience buddies" for peer support.
    - Bring in a coach or facilitator during intense periods.

There's No Such Thing as Over-Preparation

In leadership, preparation is your strongest competitive edge. It's what keeps chaos in check, ensures consistency under pressure, and signals respect for everyone's time, especially in high-stakes environments.

Before any client meeting or company-wide all-hands, I insist on internal alignment. We don't just show up, we rehearse. Multiple times if needed. We get the messaging clear, scripts sorted, decks sharp, and most importantly, the flow practiced. Who speaks after whom, how transitions happen, what each person says to set up the next, all of it is choreographed.

It's not overkill. It's discipline.

We prepare for the time we've been given, and we also prepare for what happens if things change. What if the client takes longer in their intro? What if they want to talk more before we even begin? That's where Plan B kicks in. A 15-minute demo will also have a 5-minute version, sharp and tight, ready to go.

No scrambling. No panic. Just smooth execution, because we saw it coming.

This level of preparation might look excessive to outsiders. But it's what keeps us professional, composed, and effective, even when the situation shifts. And in leadership, that's exactly what people expect from you: clarity under pressure.

And here's something I've consistently observed: After such meetings, it rarely feels like a win. It doesn't feel like a "big moment" or a dramatic turning point. Instead, it feels like we've executed the next step of a well-planned process. Calm. Controlled. No surprises. And that's exactly how it should feel.

Great leadership isn't built on adrenaline highs. It's built on steady, methodical progress. When preparation is thorough, the output is predictable, and that's the real win.

Final Word

Setbacks are not failures of character; they are moments of truth. How a team metabolizes a loss can shape its entire trajectory. As a leader, your role is not to protect the team from pain but to create the conditions where pain can be processed with dignity, clarity, and courage. This toolkit gives you practical rituals, language, and structures to do just that. Use it flexibly and often.

Chapter 5: Move from Control to Trust

The Role of Autonomy in Creating True Team Ownership

Trust. It is a little word whose definition leads either to the success or failure of all teams. You can have the best processes, high-tech tools, and the best brains in the world, but without trust, it all appears like you are building on sand.

So, the question I get asked a lot is: But how do I know who I can trust on my team? The question tends to come from leaders who have gotten burned in the past, a missed deadline, a careless error, or a promise that vanished under pressure. And the reality is, there isn't a formula that will work all the time. Trust isn't a spreadsheet equation; it's a relationship forged over time.

But. There are some patterns that you begin to see when you work directly with individuals.

Three things come to mind for me.

First, discipline. If I get a commitment from someone to have a task done by Friday, I pay attention to whether it shows up on Friday, not Monday, with apologies, not "nearly there" on Friday. Individuals who consistently keep their word, even when things become difficult, lay the groundwork for trust. Discipline does not equal rigidity; it equals the capacity to make commitments and come through on them.

Second, attitude. I will be confident in a team member who walks into a meeting with positive energy and is ready to tackle the most serious assignments without drama. It is not that you cheer the loudest in the crowd, but you radiate a "we just will work it out" attitude. Attitude influences the emotional tone in a team, and in strenuous situations, the tone is as important as technical qualities.

Third, curiosity. There are naturally curious people, in whom I believe. They tell us, "Why must we do it that way?" not that things are bad, but so we can really understand and improve them. They probe further and ask the surrounding and do not give up until they receive an answer. Curiosity is an indicator of ownership since the interested and curious are not concerned about the tasks put in front of them.

When you have to deal with individuals who are all these traits: disciplined, positive, and inquisitive, you start to feel that little green light of confidence that cannot be expressed in words: I can depend on this individual. And when you've got deep trust, something magical occurs; you can back off, relax your grip, and let people operate independently.

The Power (and Fear) of Letting Go

Here's the uncomfortable reality: stepping out of control into trust is a frightening prospect. For most leaders, control is comforting. You can manage every detail, review every deliverable, and approve every decision. Maybe it's draining your energy, but at least you sense you're in control.

But here's the paradox: the more you control, the less ownership your people feel. When every decision must go through you, your people begin to act like passengers, not drivers. They wait for direction, follow the letter of the plan, and cease to think for themselves. And in the long term, that kills innovation.

I personally found out the difficult way some time ago during my trying leadership years. I was in charge of the implementation of an important project for a well-known client, and I was not willing to watch it fail. I reviewed each and every presentation as well as triple-checked every number and went to all meetings. Fingerprints of mine were on all of the slides. The project was completed successfully, on time, on schedule, with glowing testimonies from the client. And still there was a feeling that something was not right.

The feedback that I received when I asked the team what they thought of the project was polite but distant. "It went fine." "Pleased it is finished." No one showed pride or enthusiasm. I had reached perfection, but my perfection, not theirs. Reality struck me: I hadn't created ownership; I had created dependency.

Autonomy: The Catalyst for Ownership

Autonomy is the cure for control. When individuals are given the ability to make choices about how to accomplish something, they begin to own their work in a real way. They do more thinking for themselves, take more intelligent risks, and have a deeper sense of ownership in the results.

But autonomy is not abdication. It's not about putting folks into the deep end and hoping they make it. It's about designing a system in which freedom and responsibility work together. Here's what that means in practice:

Have clear outcomes, not specific instructions. Rather than specifying exactly what needs to be done, specify what success is and leave the pathway to the team. For instance: "We require a marketing campaign that brings 20% more sign-ups in three months" is more liberating than "We require three Instagram ads, two blog posts, and one webinar."

Establish boundaries of decision-making. Autonomy is most effective when individuals understand the limits of their authority. Perhaps they can make every operational decision within a given budget, but beyond that, there needs to be a discussion. Boundaries avoid chaos without sacrificing freedom.

Be present as a guide. Freedom of choice does not equal disappearing. The best leaders are clear: "You do this, but I'm here in case you get stuck." This balance enables individuals to attempt things their way without fearing being left behind.

Psychological Safety: Trust's Best Friend

Naturally, autonomy will only thrive if individuals feel they are secure enough to risk and share ideas. That is where psychological safety comes in: the sense of believing that you can ask questions, make errors, and say something without fear of being punished or embarrassed.

Now, there is a myth that psychological safety is about being "soft" or setting the bar lower. That's incorrect. Safety is not about shying away from accountability; it's about making space where accountability and honesty can live in harmony.

Consider this: in a low-safety setting, individuals conceal errors until it's too late, don't provide feedback openly, and play it safe rather than trying new things. In a high-safety setting, individuals voice concerns early, seek help shamelessly, and present off-the-beaten-path ideas without fear of being shot down. One of my favorites is an example from a software development team I worked with. We had a "Failure Friday" tradition, a brief, casual meeting every Friday where staff members would report one thing they goofed on that week and what they learned from it. There was no blame, no sarcasm, just curiosity. This, over time, created a culture where individuals ceased concealing mistakes and began actively looking for answers.

Funny thing, our rate of errors decreased, not because we perfected everything, but because we were transparent.

The Story: Letting Go and Watching a Team Thrive

A couple of years ago, I was driving a product launch with a young team that was relatively inexperienced. My knee-jerk reaction was to step in, direct them tightly, and avoid rookie errors. But I recalled my prior lesson: if I dictated every detail, they'd never get larger.

So, I took a different tack. I established the vision, laid out the results, and provided them with space to determine the "how." I said to them, "You have my complete trust. I'm here if you require me, but this is your production."

The first week was chaotic, ideas conflicted, timelines changed, and one key supplier backed out. I hung back, inserting myself only to pose leading questions: "What's our contingency plan?" "How will that affect the launch timeline?"

Gradually, things changed. The team ceased glancing at me for solutions and began glancing at one another. They fixed the supplier problem by negotiating a better price with a local supplier. They retooled the launch plan to allow for delays without sacrificing quality. And when the launch actually occurred, it was a huge success, not because it was perfect, but because it was theirs.

The pride on their faces that day told me everything I needed to know: ownership changes everything.

Inclusion and Shared Power

If autonomy is the engine, inclusion is the fuel. A team succeeds when every voice has room at the table, not the loudest or most experienced, but every voice. Shared power doesn't equate to every decision being a consensus; it equates to everyone's view being heard and considered. I've seen the innovation gap that happens when inclusion is missing. In one organization, a product team was designing a mobile app targeted at first-time internet users in rural areas. The meetings were dominated by urban, tech-savvy voices; no one thought to ask the customer service reps who actually spoke with rural users daily. When we finally incorporated those reps into the discussion, they brought up usability problems that nobody had seen.

The product was better overnight. Inclusion is more than a feel-good philosophy; it's a business differentiator. Diverse ideas challenge assumptions, identify blind spots, and unlock innovation. But inclusion doesn't just happen by chance; it occurs when leaders proactively invite and amplify others' perspectives.

Defining a High-Performance Culture in a Team Environment

When individuals speak of "high-performance teams," it tends to sound like buzzword nonsense. But when you take away the corporate speak, what it actually means is a team of individuals who've made excellence a practice, not an exception. These are not teams that only hit objectives; they set the bar for themselves higher, over and over, regardless of how high they already are.

The roots of such a culture are a mindset, namely, a growth mindset. That is the quiet conviction, secretly, that skills can be created by effort, learning, and persistence. It's the inability to accept that skills are fixed, talent is something you're born with, or that success happens once. In a growth-mindset team, the discussion is never "we've arrived." It's always "what's next, and how do we get there?

What a Growth Mindset Looks Like in Action

If you walked into a meeting of a high-performance team, you'd pick up on something immediately.

First, there is a sense of openness in the room. Individuals voice opinions without worrying about being shut down. Even when they're demonstrated to be beating expectations, the conversation isn't a congratulatory backslapper but rather discussing what can be done differently. A sales team that's just had a record quarter may still spend 80% of their meeting tearing apart where deals may have been closed more quickly, or how client satisfaction scores may have been higher.

They aren't pursuing perfection because they're insecure; they're driven by curiosity. They really do want to know how far they can push it, how many ways they can come up with to solve a problem, and how they can improve tomorrow's results compared to yesterdays.

This isn't to say they exist in a state of chronic discontent. Far from it. High-performance culture is well aware of how to celebrate victories without allowing them to propagate complacency. The champagne corks are popping on Friday night, yet come Monday morning, they're already standing around and saying: "Okay, okay, how do we take this and make it better?"

The Flexibility Factor

One of the most underrated attributes of a high-performance team is flexibility, not in the "work from anywhere" sense but in the ability to adjust based on new learnings.

It is simple for teams to become stuck in the way that they have always done things, particularly if that way has proven to be effective before. Yet high performers view past success as a point of reference, rather than as a guide. They understand that what worked previously may not work now, and what works today might not work in the future.

Imagine it as a championship-winning sports team. They don't enter the next season running the same game plan because it worked last time. Opponents adapt. The environment adapts. The rules occasionally change. So they learn the game anew, reinvent their strategies, and emerge stronger, not despite change, but because of it.

This adaptability means they're rarely blindsided by disruption. They may not predict every change, but they've built the muscles to respond fast.

Conversations That Drive Growth

In many organizations, meetings are status updates. In high-performance cultures, meetings are laboratories for ideas. The goal isn't to tick boxes, it's to push thinking further.

In a team with a growth mindset, you'll hear questions like:

"If we began this project from scratch today, how would we do it differently?"

"What's the one thing we're avoiding because it's painful to discuss?"

"Where are we misjudging our strengths, and underestimating our threats?"

"What can we take away from the last error that we haven't implemented yet?"

These are not nitpicking questions; they're about ensuring the team is never driving on autopilot. Over time, this mentality changes the team's default mindset from defensive ("let's keep what we have") to proactive ("let's build what we want").

Trust: The Invisible Fuel

All of this requires trust.

High-performance cultures are founded on the assumption that each member is entitled to challenge concepts without taking it personally. Individuals do not conceal failures; instead, they bring them up immediately so that they can be corrected and learned from. Leaders do not penalize failure where it originates from experimentation; they penalize indifference.

This trust is not something you can create at a one-day team-building retreat. It's created through repeated loops of showing up, following through, and having each other's backs, even when things fall apart. It becomes the glue that holds the team together over time through both wins and losses.

Beyond the Numbers

High performance is often gauged in most organizations solely by numbers, sales closed, units shipped, and deadlines achieved. But in a real high-performance culture, the how is as important as the what.

A group that achieves every goal but exhausts its employees, disregards learning, or suppresses creativity isn't really high-performing; it's merely high-output. The distinction is nuanced yet significant: high performance is sustainable, high output is not.

The leaders in such settings realize that sustained greatness demands equilibrium. They will spend money on training, mental health, and competence building, not because it sounds great on paper, but because they understand that it is the only way to continue to get better year after year.

Leadership's Role in Shaping the Culture

Leaders establish the emotional and strategic tone of a team. In an atmosphere of high performance, leaders are coaches, not commanders. They believe their role is to establish a climate where people feel they can take risks, stretch, and where potential is cultivated relentlessly.

It means seeing effort alongside achievement. It means asking "What did you learn?" even when the response to "Did it work?" is "No." It means evidencing the same curiosity, humility, and flexibility that they demand from their teams.

When leaders lead by example in their own learning process, opening up both successes and failures, it communicates to the team that growth is a shared experience rather than a mandate imposed from the top.

Why It's Uncommon, and So Worth Creating

Here's the reality: high-performance cultures are uncommon because they're difficult to maintain. They take more than a mission statement on the wall. They need ongoing attention, intentional hiring, consistent reinforcement, and leaders who are willing to put in the effort.

But when you do it well, the reward is tremendous. Not only in performance, but in motivation, in retention, and in the simple job satisfaction people have when they know they're working on something truly special.

A high-performing team not only produces exceptional outcomes, but it also forms the type of careers and experiences that people later in their lives look back on as the highlight of their careers.

And maybe most indicative of such a culture? Even after the project is complete, the goals are achieved, and the cheering dies down, the individuals in it continue to carry the mindset forward, onto new teams, new organizations, and new challenges. Because once you've been in an organization that believes in growth, you can't help but see its impact.

The Cost of Ego in Leadership

I've seen ego do some pretty spectacular things in leadership. And I've seen it wreck things beyond repair.

It's a double-edged sword, sharp enough to cut through fear and doubt, but just as capable of cutting down trust, relationships, and opportunities if it's swung recklessly.

When people ask me, "Isn't ego a bad thing for a leader?" I always say, "Not necessarily."

Without some ego, you don't push limits. You don't stand up for your ideas. You don't walk into rooms where you're the youngest, least experienced person and still speak up. Ego, when healthy, fuels confidence, ambition, and the courage to take calculated risks.

But here's the trouble, ego is a bit like salt. A pinch brings out the flavour. Too much and the whole dish is ruined.

The Fine Line Between Confidence and Arrogance

Every leader I've ever respected had an ego. That's how they got there in the first place.

You don't reach the top by being timid. You reach it by believing you can, sometimes even when others don't. That belief comes with a certain self-assuredness, an inner voice that says, "I can do this. I'm built for this."

But here's the danger:

Confidence says, "I can do this."

Arrogance says, "Only I can do this."

The shift from one to the other can be so subtle that you don't even notice it's happened until you've alienated your team or lost perspective.

I've been there myself, moments where my conviction turned into stubbornness, where "standing my ground" became "refusing to listen."

The cost? Good ideas that never saw the light of day because I thought mine was better. Relationships were strained because I couldn't admit I was wrong. Projects that moved more slowly because I resisted change.

When Ego Starts Chasing Applause

One of the sneakiest traps ego sets is redirecting your ambition from genuine goals to external validation.

It's not about what you want anymore; it's about what others will think when you achieve it.

You start chasing the corner office, not because it's where you can make the most impact, but because it looks impressive.

You take on projects you don't care about because they'll bring public praise.

Your "why" stops being personal and starts being performative.

The problem is that applause fades quickly. You'll hit a milestone, get the recognition, feel good for about three days... and then you're restless again.

I've watched leaders get caught in this cycle, constantly trying to top their last achievement, never satisfied, always looking over their shoulder to see who's watching.

The Hidden Costs of Ego

Ego in leadership doesn't just impact you. It ripples outward.

Here's what it can cost, and I'm not just talking in financial terms.

1. The Cost to Decision-Making

When ego drives, you stop making decisions based on facts and start making them to protect your image.

You avoid admitting mistakes because you think it'll make you look weak.

You double down on bad ideas because changing course would feel like losing.

And slowly, you start confusing being right with doing right.

2. The Cost to Relationships

A leader's greatest currency is trust.

When ego runs unchecked, that trust erodes.

Your team stops bringing you bad news because they're afraid of your reaction.

Peers stop giving you honest feedback because they know you won't hear it.

Before long, you're leading in a bubble, cut off from the reality you need to make good calls.

3. The Cost to Growth

If ego tells you, "I already know," then curiosity dies.

You stop learning.

You stop asking questions.

You stop listening to people who are younger, newer, or less "accomplished" than you, even though they might have the freshest ideas in the room.

My Wake-Up Call

I'll never forget the meeting that humbled me.

I was leading a high-stakes project, and my team was trying to convince me to take a different approach. I'd already invested weeks in my original plan and couldn't stomach the idea of scrapping it. So, I shut them down. Firmly. Almost dismissively.

Three months later, the project flopped. The market had shifted, and my plan was outdated before we even launched. The painful part wasn't the failure; it was the realisation that my team had seen it coming. They had tried to warn me. But I was too wrapped up in my own certainty to hear them. That day, I learned that ego doesn't just cost you mistakes, it costs you the chance to avoid them.

Balancing Ego With Self-Awareness

The best leaders I've known have one thing in common: high emotional intelligence.

They know when their ego is whispering, "Don't back down," and when humility needs to say, "Listen."

Here's how they balance it:

- They separate their ideas from their identity. If someone critiques their idea, they don't take it as a personal attack.
- They invite challenge. They build teams with people who will speak up, even when it's uncomfortable.
- They reflect often. They make time to ask themselves, "Am I making this decision because it's right, or because it makes me look right?"

The Quiet Power of Humility

Humility isn't about downplaying your achievements or pretending you don't know your worth.

It's about recognising that your worth doesn't depend on always being the smartest person in the room.

A humble leader will say, "I don't have all the answers, but I know how to find them."

They'll step back so someone else can step forward.

They'll share credit, even when they could easily take it.

And here's the irony, that humility only makes their leadership stronger.

When Ego Serves You Well

Let's not forget, ego can be a powerful ally.

The same force that pushes you to speak up in a tense boardroom is the one that fuels late nights and tough calls.

It's the little spark that says, "Why not me?" when an opportunity comes up that others think is out of reach.

The key is to treat ego like a strong but unpredictable horse; you hold the reins, not the other way around.

Let it run when you need speed and courage. Pull back when it starts veering off course.

Questions Leaders Should Ask Themselves

If you want to know whether your ego is helping or hurting you, try asking:

- Would I still make this choice if no one knew about it?
- Am I protecting my idea or protecting my image?
- Have I given my team a real chance to disagree with me?
- When was the last time I changed my mind because someone else had a better idea?

The Long-Term Game

The ego loves quick wins and visible victories. But leadership is a long-term game. Sometimes the smartest move is the one that gets zero applause in the short term but sets your team up for years of success. That requires patience, trust, and a willingness to be wrong in public so you can be right in the long run. The truth is, the ego will always be part of leadership. You can't, and shouldn't, try to erase it.

The goal is to manage it. To use it as fuel without letting it burn the very ground you're trying to build on. Because when you get it right, ego doesn't just serve you. It serves the people you lead, the vision you're building, and the legacy you leave behind.

When Ego Consumes the Win

Fresh off a multi-million-dollar venture capital raise, our organization was at an inflection point.

We had every reason to feel invincible.

Investors believed in our IP.

Early customers were leaning in, excited about what we could offer. The market winds felt like they were at our backs. This funding was meant to be our catalyst, the moment we could accelerate product development, strengthen our brand, and seize market share with both speed and precision. For months, we had lived in a state of possibility, of "when we get the raise..." thinking. Now, the money was in the bank. It was time to turn possibility into execution.

But the story didn't unfold as we imagined.

Instead of becoming the launchpad we envisioned, the funding became the start of our unraveling.

The Charisma Trap

At the center of this chapter in our company's history was a strong-willed, ego-driven sales leader. Charismatic. Articulate. Confident to the point of being magnetic.

He had a gift, the ability to sell a vision in a way that made people believe not just in the product, but in the inevitability of its success. He could walk into a room of skeptical investors and have them leaning forward within minutes.

To his credit, he played an instrumental role in getting us to the fundraising table. His relentless optimism and persuasive energy helped us close a round that many thought was out of reach. In the fundraising stage, he was an asset we couldn't have done without.

The problem? He couldn't shift gears.

Fundraising is about selling the dream.

Running the business is about building reality. And those are very different skill sets.

When the Money Arrives

The moment the funding came in, so did the internal power plays. No longer was the conversation about how "we" would grow. It became about how "his team", sales, would dominate the allocation of funds.

His argument was simple: sales drive everything. Without aggressive market penetration, he claimed, product improvements were irrelevant. Why polish what you can't sell? Why slow down for refinements when you can flood the market first?

The logic sounded compelling in a vacuum. But we weren't operating in a vacuum; we were operating with an early-stage product that still had stability issues, a brand with limited awareness, and a customer base that needed nurturing as much as expansion.

From Strategy to Turf War

The leadership team's conversations quickly stopped being about strategy and started being about territory.

Our product leaders pleaded for time and resources to strengthen our IP. They knew that without scalability and resilience, any surge in sales would collapse under its own weight.

The brand team, meanwhile, pushed hard for investment in customer education and positioning. We were battling competitors with more polished offerings and better recall. Without improving perception, the long-term cost of customer acquisition would keep climbing.

But these discussions rarely went anywhere. Decisions weren't emerging from healthy debate; they were being dictated through dominance. Meetings became charged, sometimes outright hostile. People started positioning themselves not as collaborators but as defenders of their department's survival.

Ego as the Operating System

It didn't take long for ego to replace strategy as our default mode of operation.

Data took a back seat to opinion.

Alignment took a back seat to individual wins. Short-term wins became the measuring stick, even when they came at the expense of long-term resilience. In hindsight, the most dangerous assumption we made was that vision, even without substance, could be sustained by charisma. And for a short while, it seemed to work.

We posted impressive top-line numbers in the early months after the raise. They were driven almost entirely by the aggressive selling of promise and potential. On the surface, the graphs looked great.

But the cracks were already forming.

When the Dream Meets the Market

As the product went from pitch decks to real-world use, the questions from prospects got sharper.

How does this integrate with our existing systems?

What's the uptime guarantee?

How do you handle scale under load?

The truth was, we didn't have strong enough answers. Our product team had been starved of resources to shore up exactly these areas. The sales machine kept moving, but the conversion rate from demo to signed deal began to drop.

Competitors who had invested more steadily in product and brand started catching up, then overtaking us. Their offerings were more stable, their messaging clearer. And suddenly, our charm offensive wasn't enough.

The Human Cost

The internal impact was even more corrosive than the market impact.

Morale began to slide.

The sense of shared mission, the "us against the world" spirit that had carried us through the lean days, was replaced by quiet cynicism. Departments stopped trusting each other. Sales saw the product as a bottleneck. Product saw sales as reckless. Brand felt unheard entirely.

The most talented people, the ones who could have helped us turn the ship around, began to leave. Some went to competitors. Others simply burned out and stepped away from the industry for a while.

We were losing not just customers, but capability.

Investors Lose Patience

Investors can be patient when they believe in the trajectory. They can forgive early stumbles if they see a clear, disciplined path forward.

But we weren't showing discipline. We weren't showing unity. And our numbers, once impressive, began to stall.

The promised "hockey stick" growth curve never materialized. Instead, our performance plateaued, then started to dip.

When investors pressed for answers, we gave them the same kind of glossy optimism that had worked in the fundraising stage. But they were no longer buying the dream; they wanted proof of reality.

That proof wasn't there.

How Ego Kills Potential

Looking back, our downfall wasn't because we lacked talent, funding, or opportunity.

We had all three in abundance.

What we lacked was the humility to integrate perspectives, the patience to build a foundation before chasing scale, and the discipline to make decisions based on the company's long-term health rather than individual power plays.

Ego overruled strategy.

Control replaced collaboration.

And the business paid the price.

The Leadership Lessons

If there's one thing I took from this experience, it's that raising money doesn't solve cultural issues; it amplifies them.

If there are fractures in trust, those fractures will widen when the stakes are higher.

If there's an imbalance in decision-making, that imbalance will become more visible and more damaging when more resources are in play.

Here's what I wish I had done sooner:

- Re-centered decision-making on shared goals. Before the funds even hit the account, we should have aligned, in writing, on how they would be deployed in a balance between growth and resilience.
- Set clear accountability for cross-functional success. No single department "owns" growth. Revenue without retention isn't growth. A brand without a product isn't growth. Product without adoption isn't growth.
- Addressed ego head-on. We danced around it, hoping it would resolve itself. It never does.

- Protected the foundation. Scaling a weak foundation doesn't make it strong; it makes the cracks more dangerous.

The Hard Truth

When a leader's ego goes unchecked, it doesn't just harm relationships; it changes the organization's DNA. Decisions start being made for the leader's benefit rather than the companies. People stop speaking up because they know it won't matter. And soon, the only thing that truly grows is the distance between what you could have been and what you are.

Our company never fully recovered. We didn't implode overnight; it was more like a slow leak of talent, trust, and relevance until there was nothing left to hold us together.

It was painful to watch, and even more painful to know it was avoidable.

Toolbox

<u>1. Delegation Map: Urgent / Important / Ownership</u>

Draw a simple 3-column table on a sheet or whiteboard. Label them Urgent, Important, and Ownership. Now, map every task on your plate into these columns.

- Urgent: Needs immediate attention, but can be delegated if you have the right trust and clarity with your team.
- Important: These tasks shape the long-term health of the team or project. Often, leaders should focus here and delegate operational urgency where possible.
- Ownership: These are non-negotiable, your personal responsibility as a leader. No one else should carry this but you.

The discipline of mapping tasks will show you where ego is making you hoard control unnecessarily. It forces a reality check: “Am I holding this because it’s best for the team, or because I want to feel important?”

2. “Build Trust in 1 Week” Challenge

Pick one trust-building behavior and overdeliver on it for 7 consecutive days. Examples:

- End every meeting by summarizing next steps and delivering on yours first.
- Give public credit daily to a team member for something they did well.
- Share a small vulnerability, a learning from a mistake, a request for help, once each day.

The goal isn't to be performative, but to create consistent signals that you are reliable, human, and invested in the team's success. When ego is managed, trust grows fast. This challenge compresses the timeline.

3. Team Canvas: Purpose – Power – Pace

Gather your team (virtual or in person) and draw three big circles labeled Purpose, Power, and Pace.

- Purpose: Why are we here? What are we trying to achieve that matters beyond targets?
- Power: What strengths, resources, and decision rights do we have to make this happen? Are they distributed well?
- Pace: How fast do we need to move, and what rhythms (daily stand-ups, weekly reviews, monthly retros) keep us aligned?

When teams see the full canvas, they stop second-guessing decisions and start moving together. Leaders who share the canvas, instead of guarding it, keep ego in check and collaboration high.

Chapter 6: Light the Fire and Step Back

What do you do when you feel your own energy fading, but your team still needs you?

There is a time in each leader's path where the spark within begins to fade. You've been the well of energy, encouragement, and unrelenting drive for your people. You've been the one who ignited all-night brainstorming sessions, mobilized people toward impossible deadlines, and maintained morale when obstacles stacked up. But what do you do when you, the individual everyone turns to for fire, hit the wall?

It's easy to think that leaders have to be "on" at all times. Charisma is an unlimited reserve. That a leader is somehow immune to fatigue, stress, or bad days. The truth is, though, more basic and more prosaic: energy is a cycle. It is physical, emotional, and mental, and no one balances the three on a day-to-day basis. Leadership as an art is not invincible. It is just about getting used to being enthusiastically truthful, to set a positive example of strength to your team, and to establish systems in such a way that no one has to lose momentum when you are gone.

The Energy Equation: Physical, Emotional, Mental

Energy is not one source. It is like a tripod, bodily, emotional, and mental. If two legs of the tripod are sturdy, you may still balance. But if two are not solid, you will topple over, and the effect will be evident.

- Physical energy is a matter of rest, diet, exercise, and sleep. The human body is an engine; it cannot perform at maximum without fuel and downtime.
- Emotional energy is about mood, relationships, and morale. When you are burdened with conflict, disappointment, or personal challenges, your presence dulls, even when you're physically rested.
- Mental energy is about clarity, focus, and stimulation. You can be well-rested and happy but still feel foggy if you're loaded down or uninspired.

Leaders tend to see drops when one of these sources runs out. But consistent low energy typically signals that two or more are on empty. That is when you need to stop, recharge, and face facts, not just to yourself, but to your team.

My Travel Story: When the Body Says "Enough"

I know this from experience. After a stretch of back-to-back short travels, those 5 a.m. flights, hotel check-ins, and late-night returns, I would drag myself into the office with a hollowed body. The clock said morning, but my body said midnight. My eyes would sting from poor sleep, and even strong coffee couldn't disguise the fatigue.

Now, picture walking into a team meeting in that condition. The initial reaction for many leaders is to cover up, pretend like everything is okay, and keep pushing forward. But here's the irony: faking saps more energy than telling the truth.

So, I started practicing something that initially felt counterintuitive: calling out my energy level.

I would go into the meeting and say, "Team, I have just had three travel days in a row, and I'm not 100% today. I wanted to let you know this from the beginning so that if I don't sound as sharp, it's not about the topic, it's just my level of energy. So let's get the most critical things done today, and anything that's less critical, we'll get to tomorrow."

This tiny act of integrity accomplished two things. First, it relieved me of the pressure to "perform" when I was obviously not bringing my best self. Second, and more significantly, it granted my team permission to do the same. They noticed that even leaders are human, that it's all right to admit limitations, and that energy transparency is better than silent pretense.

The Human Signal: Permission to Be Real

When leaders model this kind of honesty, they create a ripple effect. People stop hiding their fatigue, burnout, or brain fog. They stop feeling guilty for being human. Instead, they learn to communicate openly: “I’m low today, but I’ll handle X; can someone else carry Y?”

That change is deep. It discourages unseen tension from building to disengagement. It mainstreams rest and recovery as performance. And paradoxically, it builds trust.

Because here's the reality: teams don't require perfect leaders; they require real ones. A leader who can state, "I'm not as sharp today, but collectively we can still make some headway," is much more believable than one who declares, "I'm fine" while obviously drowning.

Nano-Recovery: Little Glows of Renewal

Needless to say, integrity in itself does not fill up the tank. There are times when you just require a flash of energy to take you through the next meeting or discussion. That is where I count on what I call nano-recoveries.

Nano-recoveries are short, intentional actions, so small they might seem trivial, that restore a surprising amount of energy. They don’t replace full recovery (like sleep or downtime), but they act like sparks that reignite you for the next hour.

One of my stand-out nano-recoveries is literally taking a three- to five-minute walk down the hallway briskly. I make sure to smile, say hello, call a few names, and exchange a brief smile. That small jolt of action, coupled with the social booster of reconnecting with the people, gives me enough energy to get back into a meeting with renewed engagement.

Another trick is disrupting routine: using a different coffee on the machine, sitting in a new chair in the conference room, or switching my perspective for a bit. The brain loves novelty. If you shock it with something new, even small changes, it wakes up and adjusts.

Occasionally, I'll pick a colleague for a two-minute break, chatting about something not work-related, a football game, a new film, or even what their children are doing. The simple process of getting out of the work bubble provides me with perspective, humor, and an emotional boost.

Nano-recoveries are surprisingly straightforward, but they do great work because they remind you that energy isn't only physical. It's relational and mental, too.

Why This Matters: Energy Is Contagious

Here's the deeper reason that leaders have to watch out for their energy: energy is contagious.

When you enter a room depleted, everyone senses it. When you enter a room energized, even modestly, others reflect it. Your team doesn't require you to be a supernova of charm every day, but they do require your energy to be intentional.

This is why it is important to deal with dips and nano-recoveries honestly. It's not about being false-positive. It's about keeping your energy, whatever it is, from unwittingly dragging the team down. Rather, you learn to stabilize it, accept it, and make slight tweaks so that the group can move on.

And with time, as you continue to demonstrate this rhythm, the team learns to create its own energy anchors, rituals, peer support, humor, recognition, so that momentum doesn't crater when the leader is exhausted. That's the start of real legacy leadership: when the system operates on collective energy, not yours alone.

Reflection Point: Monitoring Your Own Energy

Stop here for a second. Reflect on the last time you noticed your energy lag.

- Was it physical fatigue, maybe from working late, traveling, or being sick?
- Was it emotional burden, stress, concern, or not feeling valued?

- Was it mental haze, too many windows open in your head, too many choices to make?

And when it did occur, what did you do? Did you buckle down and pretend your way through? Did you back away with a quietness? Or did you recognize it, make changes, and give authenticity to your team?

The manner in which you respond to these questions will not only unveil your individual energy management approach, but also the type of permission you are providing your team members. If you require perfection of yourself, they will feel compelled to reciprocate the same. If you accept humanity as the norm, they will soar in genuineness.

The Paradox of Leadership Energy

Here's the paradox I've learned: the less you fake being perpetually energetic, the more sustainable your leadership energy is. Because you are not depleting yourself by battling reality. You are going. With it, working with it, and instructing your team to do the same.

In that respect, leadership energy is not being the loudest person in the room. It's about making the environment such that energy circulates through the team, even when you're out of the way.

And that is what we will discuss in the remainder of this chapter: sustaining momentum without being the star, how to infuse rituals and rhythms that make teams aglow, and why contagious energy always wins over charisma. But it begins with this preliminary step: acknowledge your own dips, labour with them frankly, and perform nano-recoveries to remind people that you are a human being.

That, since you can only light your own, however dimly, you can direct others to do the same.

What Does Your "Recharge" Routine Look Like as a Leader?

The most underrated skill of leadership, in my view, is not strategy, not vision, not communication; it is energy management. I've come to believe that leadership is not a sprint or even a marathon; it's more like a long series of matches where you need to show up fresh, steady, and alert for each game. And the only way to do that is by creating a recharge routine that works for you.

To me, it is all about routine. Routines are believed to make life boring, but the reality is that routines give you freedom. Once you make your body and mind aware of what to expect, you will no longer waste energy on determining the little things. That energy can be used in the big decisions that matter. This is why I attempt to organize my days around some rhythms, although no two days are the same.

By the time I get up in the morning, my body is already prepared for what awaits. There is workout time, there is food time, there is time to hold longer meetings, coffee break, there is time to eat small fruits, nuts, etc., something light that will keep me going. Some days the circumstances might be different, one day it can be a board meeting, the next a client presentation, and the next day a travel, but the general trend is the same. It is this predictability that provides a form of inner balance. My body is not making an inquiry, what am I going to do next, it knows. And that

saves me from energy leaks that most people don't even realize are draining them.

Now, when it comes to the actual "charging station" of my life, sports have always been my first love. I am playing golf, badminton, tennis, and also yoga. I already have my sports plan outlined for the week, depending on which day of the week and who is able to play. It is as though it were my own little recharge calendar. And when I do not have partners around, or I am short of time, I put on my running shoes and go running 5-7km. It feels like the electric current when I am plugged in to an electric source, as the adrenaline pumps the blood, it evaporates off my skin, my feet run on the ground, the beat of my feet running on the ground. By the time I return, shower, and sit down at my desk, I feel charged enough to take on anything the day throws at me.

But here's the thing: it's not just about playing the game, it's about how you play it. Sports for me are not merely a way to burn calories or pass the time. It is my training ground for leadership. Every time I step on the court, or the golf course, or the mat, I give myself a small goal. It could be something as simple as practicing a backhand shot I've been struggling with, working on a serve in tennis, or hitting the golf ball straighter off the tee. These are small, precise, personal goals; nobody else even knows I'm doing it. But when I succeed in hitting that shot, or when I notice an improvement, there's an instant burst of energy, a sense of achievement.

I don't chase big wins on the field. I chase small, invisible wins. And this habit has slowly seeped into every other part of my life. At work, too, I constantly look for small wins, closing a tough conversation, resolving a conflict in the team, completing a piece of work before the deadline, and learning a new way to approach a problem. They may seem tiny in the moment, but when you stitch these small wins together, you begin to see momentum. And momentum is what eventually brings the big wins.

I'll give you an example. I once had a particularly tough week ahead, back-to-back investor meetings, a critical product review, and a travel schedule that left me with very little rest time. The temptation was to get overwhelmed just looking at the week's calendar. Instead, I broke it down into small wins. "If I can finish preparing the investor deck tonight, that's a win.

If I can get the product team aligned on this one feature, that's another win. If I can squeeze in a 30-minute run between two flights, that's yet another win." By the end of the week, instead of being drained, I was actually energized because I had stacked up half a dozen small victories.

Sports trained me to think this way. Every serve in tennis is an opportunity to win a point. Every hole in golf is a new chance. You don't have to win the match in one shot; you just need to keep stringing together good ones. And leadership, in many ways, is exactly like that.

There's also an element of innovation that comes with sports, and that, too, I carry into my leadership style. When you're on the field, you are forced to improvise. Maybe the wind changes on the golf course, maybe your opponent in badminton is stronger on the forehand, maybe you're too tired for your usual running pace. In those moments, you have to think differently. Try a new angle, a new rhythm, a new tactic. And when you succeed, you don't just feel the thrill of winning, you feel the satisfaction of having innovated your way out of a problem. That kind of thinking, when practiced daily on the field, becomes second nature at work.

I know some leaders prefer meditation, journaling, or long walks as their recharge routines, and those are excellent too. But for me, nothing matches the combination of physical exertion, competitive spirit, and mental strategy that sports provide. Yoga, for example, has been my anchor for calmness and balance. It complements the intensity of sports. When I practice yoga, it's not about competing or winning, it's about breathing, holding a posture, and becoming aware of how my body feels. It's my reminder that strength doesn't always have to be forceful; sometimes it comes from stillness.

So, what does my recharge routine really look like in practice? Imagine this: Monday morning, I wake up knowing I have a golf game scheduled with a friend before office hours. I focus on one specific shot I want to improve. After the game, I drive to work already feeling like I've achieved something personal. That win sets the tone for my day. Tuesday, I may have a late evening badminton game. I'll step into the court with one clear goal: to maybe control the net play better. The game is intense, and I come back sweaty, exhausted, yet deeply alive. On Wednesday, I don't have partners available, so I go for a solo 7 km run in the morning. The rhythm of the run clears my head, and by the time I shower and grab my coffee, I feel like I've already had a small victory. Thursday is yoga day, a slower, calmer, meditative recharge. Friday, I may mix it up again with tennis or another run. Weekends, if time permits, I'll go for a longer golf session.

Across the week, these activities give me microbursts of energy. They prevent me from running on empty, which is a trap many leaders fall into. I know plenty of leaders who grind through their weeks, neglecting their health, ignoring their bodies, thinking they'll "catch up on rest later." But the truth is, you can't pour from an empty cup. If you don't recharge yourself regularly, no amount of rest on the weekend can compensate.

The beauty of my recharge routine is that it also doubles up as a habit-building mechanism. Because I set small goals in sports, my brain is wired to look for small goals at work. Because I chase invisible wins in a game, I look for invisible wins in meetings. And because I find energy in physical exertion, I carry that high-energy state into my interactions with the team. The ripple effect is enormous.

Sometimes people ask me, "Do you ever get tired of repeating the same routine?" My answer is: no, because the routine is the anchor, not the goal. Within the anchor, there's infinite room for variety. No two runs are the same. No two badminton matches play out identically. Even in golf, the same course feels different depending on the day. And at work, too, the routine of meetings, presentations, and decisions may look similar on the surface, but every single one brings a different challenge. The routine keeps me grounded, while the goals keep me excited.

The ultimate lesson I've learned is this: small wins create energy, energy sustains momentum, and momentum drives results. You don't need to announce these wins to the world. You don't even need external validation. All you need is the satisfaction of knowing you're improving, even if only by 1%, every single day. And when you look back after months and years, those tiny daily wins add up to a massive transformation.

That's what my recharge routine looks like. It's not glamorous, it's not complicated, and it's not even particularly unique. But it works. It works because it keeps me grounded, keeps me improving, and most importantly, keeps me energized to lead not just with strategy and vision, but with presence and vitality.

What is the Place of Reflection and Feedback in Your Leadership Development?

Had I to describe the development of leadership in one metaphor, I would refer to it as walking on a rope bridge that was put across a valley. On one end is reflection, and on the other end is feedback. You can never walk to growth if you stay on just one end. Reflection provides you with internal clarity, the inner voice that makes it possible for you to know your intent, your choices, and your values that are guiding you. Feedback, however, is the outside mirror. It gives you an idea of how people are viewing, understanding, or challenging your behavior. And sometimes both are in sync and give you the confirmation that you are doing the right thing. They sometimes run counter to one another, pulling in opposite directions, and you have to pause and think them out again, and have a rest. That's where real leadership development starts, when you can sit with both and draw lessons from their tension.

I learned that the hard way during one of our yearly sales kick-off meetings. The memory is still vivid. Last year's performance was mid-level, not catastrophic, but certainly nowhere near where we had envisioned ourselves to be. I knew we couldn't have another year of mediocrity. The agenda of the meeting was straightforward: spark a fire, establish an ambitious agenda, and charge the team to believe in what we can become. I spent hours preparing, studying market statistics, charting areas of opportunity, constructing forecasts, outlining a clean product plan, and building a narrative that connected all the dots.

It all made sense inside my head. We were going to have a robust product pipeline on the horizon, a seasoned team, a good prospect list, good market conditions, and even a respectable marketing budget. With all these pieces falling into place, we could conquer the world. My personal self-reflection was obvious: this meeting was to get the team aligned with a winning culture and to emphasize a growth focus. I was eager, even a bit impatient, to convey that message.

The day was good from where I stood. I addressed the possibilities of the future, recognized excellence, and reinforced a mindset that I frequently bore: "What have you done for us lately? " To me, it wasn't dismissive of yesterday but a reminder that business and leadership are about the future. We can't just bask in yesterday's glory; we must create tomorrow's. At the end of the session, I was satisfied.

My reflection informed me that I had succeeded: I had presented a persuasive vision for the future. Leadership, however, is never about how you feel by yourself. It is also about how the people you are leading take away with them. At breakfast the next morning, some team members casually joined me. I seized the moment and asked them how they had felt about the session. I was looking for appreciation of the vision and some energy about the roadmap.

While they did appreciate the direction and clarity, what transpired over the next hour totally flipped my perspective. They started to share their concerns, not tentatively but with forethought. It was as if they had been holding on for a window to express to me all that wasn't functioning. Inter-departmental politics, process bottlenecks, lack of training and knowledge sharing, the litany continued. I wasn't surprised because I knew all these issues already.

What did come as a surprise to me was that they were so willing to raise it in detail, and their disappointment with me for not taking up these issues during the session.

In my head, the meeting was all about mobilizing the team towards possibilities. In their head, it was a chance to get past the broken things before jumping into new stuff. Both thoughts were okay; neither was bad. But having the focus misaligned meant that when I was toasting our future, they were still in the pain of the moment.

It taught me one of the greatest lessons in leadership development: reflection without feedback can be a blind spot, and feedback without reflection can be noise. Development is in the balance of both.

Reflection: The Leader's Internal Compass

Reflection is where leadership starts. It's your capacity to stop, turn inward, and interrogate yourself with the hard questions: Why did I make that decision? What values was I operating from? How did I present myself in that meeting? Did I act on conviction or ego? Reflection is the gyroscope that keeps you anchored to your purpose. Without it, leadership turns reactive, running after results without knowing the "why" behind them.

But reflection only gets you so far. It is subjective and personal. You can reflect and decide that you aced a situation when, in fact, the folks around you felt totally disconnected. My kick-off meeting was like that. Reflecting, I believed I had inspired the team. Without feedback, I'd have kept believing that.

Feedback: The External Mirror

That is where feedback comes into play. Feedback informs you how your intention is turning into influence. You may feel that you are inspiring, but your team might be feeling pressured. You might feel that you are being transparent, but they might hear ambiguity. Feedback is that mirror which enables you to view what you are unable to do on your own.

But even feedback has limits. It can be tinted, coloured through the other person's perspective, their mood, their life experiences. Feedback, at times, will be more about the giver than about you. That's why it cannot be blindly accepted; it must be put alongside reflection.

Together, reflection and feedback form a cycle of growth. Reflection aids you in processing feedback, filtering signal and noise, and tuning it to your inner compass. Feedback on its part will assist you in verifying the effectiveness of your reflection, confront your assumptions, and unveil blind spots of which you were unaware.

Reflection Without Feedback = Self-Delusion

Just think if I had left that sales meeting feeling, "That was perfect, the team is aligned." Had there been no breakfast conversation, I would have continued with misplaced assurance. Reflection can sometimes lead you to believe that your intentions were sufficient, that your reasoning was rational. Leadership is not a matter of what you say; it's a matter of what people hear.

Feedback Without Reflection = Confusion

Concurrently, if I had just soaked up all that was said by my team during breakfast without thinking, I would have been drowning. Should I give up on my vision because they were centered on issues? Should I shift all my focus to making processes right before discussing growth? Feedback without thinking results in reactive leadership; you keep on adjusting to every feedback without a reference point. That's just as risky.

The Real Growth: Balancing Both

The actual growth is in interlacing the two. For me, the learning was not to pick between visioning and problem-solving but to balance them. I understood that while it was necessary to present the team with a thrilling horizon ahead, it was also necessary to recognize the difficulties holding them back. A balanced message would have been: "Yes, we have a robust product pipeline and an enormous market opportunity in front of us. But first, let's also tackle the hurdles holding us back.

Together, we can solve these problems while striving for growth." That balance would have made the team feel heard and still motivated.

Over time, I developed the practice of looking back at feedback to see patterns. Rather than taking each comment as an isolated response, I'd take a step back and question: Are multiple people holding the same opinion? Is it consistent criticism over a period of time? If so, then there is indeed a blind spot I need to address. If not, it could be just someone's opinion.

Similarly, I habituated myself to reflect on a regular basis, even without feedback. It is dangerous to wait for feedback to determine how you are doing. Sometimes people do not tell you the truth, sometimes they sweet-talk, and sometimes they do not even bother. That is why you have to develop your own reflection system, journaling, debriefing after a meeting, and checking with yourself what you might have done differently.

And lastly, I learned to ask for feedback intentionally to challenge the accuracy of my self-reflection. If I sensed that a meeting went well, I would ask a trusted teammate, "Did it land the way I thought it did?" If I were uncertain, I would ask, "What's one thing I could have done differently?" Small, direct questions tend to elicit the most valuable feedback.

Leadership as a Rope Between Two Poles

This is why I return to the metaphor of reflection and feedback as two ends of a rope: You must hold both in order to balance. Pull too hard on reflection, and you exist in your head. Pull too hard on feedback, and you lose yourself.

The leadership development art is to continue walking that rope with confidence, understanding that both ends are required, even when they pull in opposite directions.

Reflecting on that sales kickoff, I'm thankful that it unfolded as it did. Because it provided me with an experience I still call on years later. It taught me that leadership has nothing to do with perfect messages or faultless strategies. It is about deeply listening, genuinely reflecting, and adapting with ease. It's about understanding that your growth is as much in how you deal with criticism as in how you imagine the future. That morning at breakfast, my team unwittingly provided me with one of the greatest gifts: they demonstrated how my reflection needed to be tested against reality. And conversely, my reflection enabled me to sift their input into something constructive without forgetting the vision. That rope, pulled between reflection and feedback, was the bridge that I still traverse today as a leader.

What Do You Hope Your Team Remembers About Working With You Five Years From Now?

When I think about the legacy, I want to leave with every team I've worked with, the answer comes back to two words that I've always carried with me: powered on. To me, being powered on is not just about enthusiasm or energy in bursts. It's about creating a sustained state of innovation, curiosity, and involvement. It is about having the courage to challenge the status quo while keeping your purpose clear and your customer at the center of your decisions.

If five years from now, my former team members pause during a brainstorming session at some new company and think, "This is exactly what it means to be powered on", then I would feel I have done my job as a leader. I don't want to be remembered for titles, hierarchy, or authority. Those things fade. What endures is the culture we create together, the mindset we share, and the courage we cultivate to push past the ordinary.

Powered On: A State of Mind

Every team has its highs and lows. There are days when everything feels like it's falling into place, and others when no strategy seems to land. The "powered on" mindset is about showing up the same way in both situations, with energy, creativity, and a willingness to learn.

I've often told my team that our real enemy is not competition or external pressure. It's lethargy. It's when we start thinking in silos, focusing on titles or reporting lines, or when we allow the weight of process to crush the spark of innovation. Being powered on means having the mental courage to break those boundaries.

I have never let my job title confine me. If I felt something was right for the customer, the organization, or the team, I crossed mental boundaries to push for it. I want my people to remember that this freedom is not only allowed, it is expected. Titles exist to give structure, not to build walls.

Beyond Metrics: Meaning as the Anchor

One of the things I've learned is that people rarely remember the numbers five years later. They don't sit back and say, "Yes, 2019 was the year we hit 128% of our quarterly targets." They remember how they felt when they achieved something that mattered. They remember the late-night brainstorming sessions when the energy was palpable. They remember that sense of alignment when the whole team rallied around a common purpose.

So if my teams remember me for anything, I hope it is for always asking the "why" questions. Why does this matter to the customer? Why does this solve a real problem? Why does this align with our purpose? I've always pushed for progress to be measured not just by metrics but by meaning.

And that brings me to one of the most underrated tools I use as a leader: the Purpose Retrospective.

Toolbox 1: Purpose Retrospective – Reviewing Progress Beyond Numbers

In traditional retrospectives, teams look at what went well, what didn't, and what needs to improve. But I like to add a layer that goes deeper: Did this project add meaning to what we're doing? Did we grow in a way that mattered?

A Purpose Retrospective involves asking three simple but powerful questions:

1. Impact – Who benefited from what we built?
2. Meaning – Did it align with our larger purpose?
3. Growth – Did this stretch us in ways that built new capabilities?

I've used this with product teams, service teams, and even sales groups. At first, it feels strange to step away from numbers, but soon people realize that purpose gives numbers their real weight.

Five years from now, if a team member remembers that I constantly asked them to think beyond metrics and look for meaning, then I know I've planted the right seeds.

Creating Habits That Outlive You

Culture is not built in a day. It's built into habits. And as leaders, we often underestimate how much influence we have in shaping daily practices that linger long after we leave.

That's why I've always been a big believer in structured habit loops for teams. When people do something consistently, it starts to rewire the way they think.

This is where my 30–60–90 Plan for Habit Loops comes in.

Toolbox 2: The 30–60–90 Plan – Building Team Habit Loops

When a new initiative starts or a new leader join, the first 90 days are crucial. I use this framework not just for onboarding but for shaping culture:

- First 30 days – Create clarity. The team defines the habit they want to build. For example: "We will start every meeting with a customer story" or "We will end every week with one learning reflection."
- Next 60 days – Practice consistency. The leader ensures it's happening every time, without fail. The team sees the rhythm forming.
- By 90 days, it becomes automatic. The habit doesn't feel forced anymore; it becomes part of the team's DNA.

I've seen this work wonders. One sales team I led started with a habit of sharing "one failure and one fix" every Friday. Initially, it felt awkward. By the 60-day mark, it became second nature. By 90 days, people were volunteering stories without hesitation. The result? A fearless culture where learning was normalized.

When I think about legacy, this is what I want: teams that develop habits strong enough to survive without me. If five years later, they're still practicing a ritual we built together, they'll remember not me, but the value of staying powered on.

The Power On Culture: A Framework

At the heart of all this is what I call the Power On Culture Framework, a simple model that combines three elements:

1. Innovation – Not waiting for permission to think differently.
2. Involvement – Every voice matters; titles don't define contribution.
3. Inquisitiveness – Asking "why" and "what if" more than "can we?"

Whenever I've embedded this framework in a team, I've seen transformation. People start challenging outdated processes. They become bolder in experimenting. They involve each other without ego or hierarchy.

For instance, I remember a project where the youngest member of the team, just six months out of college, suggested a customer-first tweak that none of us had thought of. In a hierarchical culture, her voice may never have been heard. But in a powered-on culture, her idea was not only accepted but celebrated. That single change saved us thousands of dollars and months of wasted effort.

Toolbox 3: The Power On Culture Framework

To put this into practice, I ask my teams to constantly evaluate themselves on three questions:

- Innovation – Did we try something new this week?
- Involvement – Did every voice in the room get heard?
- Inquisitiveness – Did we ask at least one question that challenged our assumptions?

If the answer is yes across all three, then the team is powered on. If not, we know exactly where we need to push harder.

Memory Is Built on Emotion

People don't remember dry meetings or sterile processes. They remember the moments that stirred something inside them. That's why I've always tried to bring energy into the room.

Whether it was brainstorming with music playing in the background, celebrating small wins with unplanned pizza nights, or turning setbacks into teachable moments, my goal was to make work feel alive.

Five years from now, I don't expect people to recall the exact campaigns we ran or the numbers we achieved. But I do hope they remember the feeling of being fully engaged, fully alive, powered on.

Leadership Without Titles

One of the deepest impressions I want to leave is that leadership is not tied to designation. Anyone can lead from wherever they are if they have the courage to speak up, the humility to listen, and the persistence to act.

I've seen interns inspire CEOs. I've seen frontline staff shift organizational strategy with a single customer story. If people who worked with me remember that they don't need a title to lead, then I know they'll carry that lesson into every room they enter for the rest of their careers.

The Legacy I Hope to Leave

So, what do I want my team to remember about me five years from now? Not that I was their "boss." Not that I ran a tight ship. I want them to remember the feeling of being powered on.

I want them to remember that titles never stood in the way of doing the right thing. That challenging the status quo was not only accepted but encouraged. Innovation, involvement, and inquisitiveness were the cornerstones of everything we did.

If they look back and say, "Working with you taught me how to stay powered on, no matter the circumstance," then that is legacy enough.

Verses Kindler Publication

Verses Kindler Publication

Reach us through our website

https://www.verseskindlerpublication.com/

For more information visit our Instagram or Facebook page.